FLOWERS
in the
KITCHEN

A Bouquet
of Tasty Recipes

SUSAN BELSINGER

Photography
JOE COCA

INTERWEAVE PRESS

The flowers presented in this book are edible and not harmful to the ordinary individual. Some flowers, however, are poisonous; and some may cause allergic reactions in susceptible individuals, as any foods might. If you react negatively to any edible flower, or to any food, stop eating it immediately and consult your physician.

ON THE COVER:

'Lemon Gem' marigolds garnish a simple dish of pasta with mushrooms and garlic.

FLOWERS IN THE KITCHEN
by Susan Belsinger
photography by Joe Coca, except as follows: Susan Belsinger, pages 29, 33, 37, 41, 49, 65, 73, 77, 81, 85, 89, 93, 97, 105, 113, 117, 125. Andrew Van Hevelingen, pages 57, 69, 121. Joanne Pavia, 109.

Design by Susan Wasinger/Signorella Graphic Arts
Production by Marc McCoy Owens and Linda Boley
Garden illustration on page 23 by Ann Sabin Swanson

Library of Congress Cataloging-in-Publication Data

Belsinger, Susan
   Flowers in the kitchen : a bouquet of tasty recipes / Susan
Belsinger ; photography by Joe Coca.
      p.   cm.
   Includes index.
   ISBN 0-934026-63-7 (pbk.) : $14.95
   1. Cookery (Flowers)   2. Flower gardening.   I. Title.
TX814.5.F5B45   1990
641.6--dc20   90-56138
                                                        CIP

First printing: 10M:291:MCA/MCA

Printed in Hong Kong; Bookbuilders Ltd

INTERWEAVE PRESS
201 East Fourth Street
Loveland, Colorado 80537

Rather appropriately, this book is for two dear friends: One is a cook who likes to garden, and the other is a gardener who likes to cook.

To Carolyn, cook and longtime kitchen cohort, whom I have spent more time with in more kitchens than I can count.

To Deborah, the flower lady, who grows and shares the loveliest flowers of anyone I know.

Acknowledgements

My hearfelt thanks go to the following people for their help in making this book:

Linda Ligon, for believing in and being so supportive of this project, as well as being an enthusiastic and honest individual and a professional editor;

My husband, Tomaso, and daughter, Lucie, for helping me while I worked on this project and for putting up with my many hours in the garden, the kitchen, and at the computer;

Thomas DeBaggio, for his herbal expertise;

Denise Doerer at the Maryland Cooperative Extension Service, Home and Garden Information Center, for her research on edible flower information;

Deborah Hall, for gathering flowers and spending hours gardening, recipe testing, and sharing her knowledge of flowers;

Peep O'Day Herb Farm in Loveland, Colorado, and Bellwether Herb Farm in Fort Collins, Colorado, for cheerfully supplying flower specimens;

Joe Coca, for his enthusiasm and fine photography;

Louanne Sargent, for her editing assistance and hours as chief cook and bottle washer par excellence;

Audrey Belsinger, Donny Hinkleman, and Marguerite Sargent, for lending props and babysitting.

TABLE OF CONTENTS

INTRODUCTION

Petals or whole blossoms of many common garden flowers add color, flavor, and drama to simple recipes.

This book is for those who love flowers and those who appreciate good food. Generally the two go hand in hand. It is for gardeners and cooks who never seem to have enough time to do the things that they like best—puttering around in the garden and creating delicious dishes in the kitchen. It offers a simple solution: grow the flowers that you enjoy, bring them into the kitchen, and eat them for supper.

People have been eating flowers since time began. Vast numbers of recipes have been recorded since ancient times using flowers in preparations from meads to meats. Some old recipes use flowers that today are considered poisonous; this book's recipes contains only flowers that taste good and are wholesome. I certainly don't want to eat bitter, strong, or metallic-tasting flowers just because they are pretty. Strange-tasting, dangerous, or questionable blooms are not included here.

The best introduction to eating flowers is to proceed with caution. Smell your flowers; aroma is a large part of taste. Take little nibbles to get to know their flavor. When serving flowers to those who are not used to eating them, don't overwhelm them with large, entire blooms. Instead, pull off petals or florets and scatter them lightly over a dish.

Be sure that you have identified your flowers correctly. Know where they come from—preferably from your own garden, or a friend's or neighbor's where you can be sure that they are unsprayed. Some grocery stores now offer edible flowers in their produce section too, along with fresh herbs and salad greens. Blooms from florists and garden centers almost always have been heavily sprayed, so they are not a good choice.

When bringing flowers in from the garden, try to leave any insects outside. Rinsing the flowers gently in a basin of cool water will flush out many of them; pat flowers dry. If you are preparing the flowers ahead of time, you can store them between slightly dampened paper towels in the refrigerator.

Using flowers in the kitchen is fun, so be creative and experiment. If you think that dill and chives go well together, then try combining their flowers in an unusual vinegar or a savory butter. Usually a combination of two kinds of flowers is enough; otherwise, the flavors can become muddied.

For best flavor, always use flowers at their peak; don't use unopened buds (with the exception of daylilies), and don't use faded or wilted flowers, as they tend to taste bitter. Be sure that blooms are free of insects; rinse and pat them dry if necessary. Never use flowers that have been sprayed with pesticides.

I want to encourage you to bring flowers out of the garden and into the kitchen. Experiment! Sample each bloom to see how it tastes and which foods it goes well with. If you don't like it, don't eat it again; if you do, plant a lot in your garden! Use flowers to add color and interest as well as new tastes to your table.

USING FLOWERS IN THE KITCHEN IS FUN, SO BE CREATIVE AND EXPERIMENT.

The flowers of coriander (also called cilantro) add a more delicate, slightly floral taste than the leaves would in this classic salsa.

WAYS WITH EDIBLE FLOWERS

Some of the nicest ways to use edible flowers are also the simplest. Garnishes of fresh-picked blossoms can turn the most mundane dish into something special: a flavorful chive blossom scattered over a simple cheese omelet, a sprinkle of violets on plain vanilla custard. Some showier blossoms can serve as surprising containers for everyday dishes. A well-seasoned chicken salad heaped into perfect tulip blossoms (with stamens removed) makes a charming presentation for a spring luncheon. Or try small scoops of fruit sherbet in gladiolus flowers for a dramatic summer dessert.

A spring salad with flowers

A well-thought-out composed salad plate is the best possible way to start or end a meal; with the addition of edible flowers, it becomes a showstopper. Flower salads are simple, delicious, and fun to create, as long as you follow a few basics. First and foremost is freshness—ingredients must be fresh, and for best flavor, in season.

As a base for your salad, choose fresh, tender lettuce leaves. Of course, homegrown, tender, tiny lettuces and other greens are the most delicious; if these aren't available, look for small heads of bibb, red leaf, oak leaf, limestone, or Boston lettuce at the market. Other tasty greens to seek are mâche, spinach, endive, chicory, rocket, radicchio, and watercress.

Herb leaves can be a nice addition. However, don't use strong-tasting ones like rosemary and sage. Basil, chervil, chives, coriander, dill, mint, parsley, and sorrel are good choices for salad herbs. Don't use too many at once—keep it to two or three.

The same rule of thumb goes for flowers in salads; don't use too many different varieties. Three to five is a good number; otherwise, the clean, fresh flavors and tastes will be lost. All of the flowers listed on the edible flower chart on pages 24–27 are good in salads. Be sure that flowers are free of insects and unsprayed.

Flowers can be picked ahead of time. Rinse and pat them dry if necessary, place them between slightly dampened paper towels, and refriger-

ate until ready to use. Though larger flowers should be separated into florets or petals, the entire bloom of small flowers can be strewn over the salad. Taste your flowers and remove any centers that seem bitter.

As for vegetable additions, you can add anything that suits your fancy, but keep it simple. In the spring, try fresh tender, steamed beets, new potatoes, or asparagus, maybe spring onions. With summer's bounty, fresh tomatoes, green beans

WITH THE ADDITION OF

EDIBLE FLOWERS, [A SALAD]

BECOMES A SHOW-STOPPER.

9

Viola, chive, and rocket blossoms add color to this spring salad.

salad combinations, colors, and tastes. Actually, most foods that ripen at the same time of year seem to go well with one another. An unlikely pairing of strawberries and watercress, both in season at the same time, results in an unusual but pleasing salad.

When combining salad greens, vegetables, herbs, and flowers, take time to picture in your mind's eye what your salad plate will look like. Then think of the flavors of your ingredients and how they will blend together. The overall effect should be a harmonious blend of flavors and palate of colors; there can be a surprise taste or two, but ingredients should not be shocking or clash with one another.

The dressing or vinaigrette should be light and uncomplicated. Pure, fruity olive oil with lemon juice or wine vinegar is the best accompaniment. Pass this alongside the salad or toss just before serving so that the flowers do not wilt.

cooked crisp-tender, and cucumbers add color and texture. Bright-colored peppers and fall fruits can enliven autumn's salad plate.

Each season will bring different

SPRING FLOWER SALAD

Wash the salad greens well and pat or spin them dry. If the leaves are large, tear them into bite-sized pieces. Wash the herbs and pat them dry. Gently rinse the flowers and pat them dry.

In a small bowl, combine the oil and vinegar with a fork, and season with salt and pepper.

Arrange the greens on a serving platter and scatter the herbs over them. Place the flowers decoratively on top. Stir the vinaigrette well and drizzle about half of it over the salad. Toss gently, add more vinaigrette if necessary, and serve immediately.

SERVES 8

About 8 cups of salad greens (baby lettuces, mâche, chicory, endive, rocket, watercress, or spinach)

About 2 cups of assorted edible flowers (apple, chervil, chive, or coriander, Johnny-jump-up, pansy, plum, scented geranium, or violet)

1 to 2 tablespoons tiny new mint leaves

2 to 3 tablespoons dill sprigs

2 tablespoons snipped chives

1/2 cup olive oil

2 to 3 tablespoons balsamic, tarragon, or herb other vinegar

Salt and freshly groundpepper

Floral jellies are delicate in flavor and color, and add a special touch to both sweet and savory dishes.

Making flower butter

A kitchen staple with a multitude of uses, flower-flavored butters can be used with bread, fish, pancakes and waffles, pasta, and every type of vegetable. Simple to make, they keep in the refrigerator for about a week. Basil, calendula, chive, coriander, dill, fennel, nasturtium, and viola flowers all lend new flavors and exciting color to food. Experiment with your favorite flowers.

To prepare 1/2 cup of flower butter, soften a stick of unsalted butter. Finely chop or shred the flowers into a chiffonade: about 2 tablespoons of flowers to 1/2 cup butter is a good ratio. Blend the flowers with the butter. You may want to add a bit of salt or pepper, lemon juice, or chopped shallots, depending on how you'll use the butter. Pack it into a ramekin or small crock and refrigerate until ready to use.

PRESERVING YOUR HARVEST

You can enjoy spring and summer flowers on your table in the dead of winter if you plan ahead a little. Flower-flavored jellies, vinegars, sugars, and teas are simple to make and make lovely gifts, too.

Flower jelly

The best flowers for making jelly are the ones with the most fragrance and flavor. Rose petals are a favorite, but petals from fruit trees such as apple, lemon, orange, or plum can be used, too. Use three cups of any of these petals for this recipe. The blossoms of anise hyssop, basil, bergamot, elder, lilac, pineapple sage, and scented geraniums are so flavorful that two cups of any of them is enough.

If the infusion seems to be a little brown or pale, add a drop or two of food coloring after straining out the flowers.

FLOWER JELLY

In a noncorrodible saucepan, bring the flowers, water, and 1/2 cup sugar to a boil. Reduce heat and simmer for 5 minutes. Remove from heat, cover, and let stand at least a few hours or overnight.

Strain flowers from syrup. Put the syrup in a large, heavy-bottomed, noncorrodible pot and add the grape juice and pectin. Bring the contents of the pot to a hard boil and boil for 1 minute.

Add the sugar all at once and stir well. Bring the contents of the pot to a full rolling boil that cannot be stirred down and boil hard for 1 minute. Remove from heat.

If desired, place a few petals or blossoms in each hot, sterilized 1/2-pint jelly jar and ladle in jelly, leaving 1/2-inch head space. Wipe the rim of the jar clean and seal with sterilized lid and ring. Cover the jars with a tea towel, away from any draft, and let cool to room temperature. Label and store jars in a cool place. If any jars have not sealed, refrigerate them and use the contents within two weeks.

*MAKES ABOUT FOUR
1/2-PINT JARS*

2 cups flower blossoms or 3
  cups flower petals (if using
  roses, snip away the bitter
  white parts)

2 cups water

1/2 cup sugar

1 cup white grape juice

1 3/4-ounce package powdered
  fruit pectin

3 cups sugar

Petals or floret for each jar, if
  desired

FLOWER VINEGARS ADD

VARIETY TO SALADS,

SAUCES, MAYONNAISE,

VEGETABLES, STIR-FRIES . . .

Flower vinegars

Flower vinegars add variety to salads, sauces, mayonnaise, vegetables, stir-fries—any dish that you might use vinegar in.

The more savory and herblike flowers work best. Anise hyssop, basil, chives, dill, fennel, lovage, marigold, marjoram, oregano, and nasturtium are good choices. The trick is to pair a chosen flower with the vinegar that will best complement its flavor without overwhelming it.

White distilled vinegar is too acid and harsh. Both the golden brown cider vinegar and malt vinegar (which is also brown) have a distinct flavor, but they might go well with some of the stronger-flavored flowers, such as chives, oregano, or sage. Red wine, sherry, and balsamic vinegar are a bit too strong-flavored for any flowers. In general, the best choices are rice wine vinegar and white wine vinegar; they are mild and slightly sweet, allowing flower flavors to come out without overpowering them. They are also very pale and will take on the color of the infused flowers.

There are two ways to infuse flowers in vinegar. In the first method, you heat the vinegar first; the second lets the sun do the work. I prefer the sun infusion because it's so easy and energy-saving, though the other method is faster.

Use clean, sterilized pint or quart canning jars. Fill them about half full of the flowers of your choice; rinse the flowers first, if necessary.

Chive blossoms impart a piquant flavor to white wine vinegar while turning it a rosy pink.

Choose the sweeter aromatic flowers to flavor sugar; anise hyssop, lavender, lilac, rose, scented geranium, and sweet violets.

For the first method, heat the vinegar in a noncorrodible pan until hot but not boiling, then pour it into the jar, leaving 1/2 inch head space, and seal. Place the jar in a warm, dark place for two weeks.

For the sun method, pour room-temperature vinegar into the jar, leaving 1/2 inch head space, and seal. Place the jar in a sunny spot outdoors or on a sunny windowsill, and let stand for three to four weeks.

After the suggested time has elapsed, strain the vinegar through cheesecloth into clean, sterilized bottles. Label them and store away from light.

Flower-scented sugars

Europeans have been making vanilla sugar for years by placing a vanilla bean in a jar of sugar. Flower-scented sugars can easily be made the same way, transforming plain sugar into a pleasing, fragrant addition to cakes, cookies, custards, whipping cream, and all sorts of sweets. Choose the sweeter aromatic flowers to flavor the sugar: anise hyssop, lavender, lilac, rose, scented geraniums, and sweet violets.

To prepare scented sugar, use a clean pint jar with a tight-fitting lid. Fill the jar about one-third full with sugar, and scatter a small handful of small flowers, florets, or petals of your choice over it. Cover the flowers with sugar so that the jar is two-thirds full, add another small handful of flowers, and cover with sugar to fill the jar, leaving about 1/2 inch head space. Put on the lid, shake the jar, and place it on a shelf in a cool, dark place. The sugar will be ready to use in two to three weeks but will become more flavorful with age. As you use the sugar, add more to take its place; it will take on the fragrance in the jar.

Drying flowers for tea

Favorite flowers can be dried to use as tea or to add to tea blends. Chamomile, hibiscus, jasmine, linden, marigold, rose, and yarrow are good candidates; they have strong, distinctive fragrances that are released on steeping. To prepare flowers for tea, pull them from their stems and spread the petals on screens or drying baskets. Place away from direct sunlight and turn occasionally until dry. If the petals have not dried

after a few days, place them on baking sheets in an oven set at about 200° F. with the door ajar. Check them every few minutes until they are crisp and completely free of moisture. Cool them and pack the dried petals into jars or tins with tight-fitting lids and store in a cool, dry place.

A teaspoon of dried flower petals steeped in a cup of freshly boiled water for 5 to 10 minutes makes a fragrant beverage.

Rose petals, lilac florets, and whole apple blossoms wreathe a creamy cheese cake.

Candying or crystallizing flower blossoms

Candied flowers are nice to have on hand to add élan to plain baked goods and other sweet treats. Top a cupcake or petit four with a single violet or rose petal, or wreathe your favorite cheesecake with all the blossoms of early spring. Good candidates for candying are apple or plum blossoms, borage flowers, lilac florets, rose petals, scented geraniums, and the violas—violets, Johnny-jump-ups, and pansy petals.

This job takes a little patience; it seems to go more quickly if you do it with a friend. The following recipe will coat quite a few flowers, but if you need more, mix up a second batch.

CANDIED FLOWER BLOSSOMS

In a small bowl, combine the egg white with the water and beat lightly with a fork or small whisk until the white just shows a few bubbles. Place the sugar in a shallow dish.

Holding a flower or petal in one hand, dip a paint brush into the egg white with the other and gently paint the flower. Cover the flower or petal completely but not excessively. Holding the flower or petal over the sugar dish, gently sprinkle sugar evenly all over on both sides. Place the flower or petal on the waxed paper to dry. Continue with the rest of the flowers.

Let the flowers dry completely; they should be free of moisture. This could take 12 to 36 hours, depending on atmospheric humidity. To hasten drying, you may place the candied flowers in an oven with a pilot light overnight, or in an oven set at 150° F to 200° F with the door ajar for a few hours.

Store the dried, candied flowers in airtight containers until ready to use. They will keep for as long as a year.

Rinsed and dried flower blossoms, separated from the stem

1 extra-large egg white, at room temperature

Few drops of water

About 1 cup superfine sugar

A small paint brush

A baking rack covered with waxed paper

M A Y   W I N E   W I T H   S W E E T   W O O D R U F F   A N D   S T R A W B E R R I E S

*MAKES ABOUT 3 QUARTS,
OR 24 PUNCH CUPS*

*1 handful of woodruff sprigs,
12 or more*

3 pints fresh, ripe strawberries

2 bottles Rhine or Moselle wine

About 1/2 cup sugar

*Woodruff sprigs and blossoms
for garnish*

*Edible flower blossoms for
garnish such as violets,
Johnny-jump-ups, pansies,
or rose petals*

1 bottle champagne

Heat the handful of woodruff sprigs on a baking sheet in a low oven for a few minutes to bring out the coumarin scent. Rinse the berries lightly and pick them over, reserving a pint of the best for garnish.

Remove the stems from the 2 pints of berries and taste the berries for sweetness. Add a pint of berries to each of two pitchers along with half the sugar if the berries are tart, less if they are sweet. Crush the berries with the sugar (a potato masher works well), and then add the woodruff, dividing it evenly. Pour a bottle of wine into each pitcher and stir well. Cover the pitchers with plastic wrap and refrigerate overnight or up to 24 hours.

To serve, strain the wine into a punch bowl. Add the ice mold, if desired. Stir in the bottle of champagne. Garnish with the reserved strawberries, woodruff, and flowers.

A spring celebration of flowers

Nothing epitomizes the pleasures of flowers in the kitchen for me more than this traditional May wine. Making the most of early spring fruits and flowers both for flavor and presentation, it's perfect for a spring tea, a wedding reception, or a baby shower. Ring your punch bowl with a delicate floral wreath, or with a riot of woodland flowers as shown here. Serve it in glass punch cups or crystal goblets.

The original recipe came from Adelma Grenier Simmons; I have adapted that basic recipe numerous times. Many punch cups later, here is my favorite version. If the weather is hot and the punch is to be out for some time, it is important to have the ingredients well chilled. Sometimes I prepare an ice mold in a ring-shaped pan to float in the punch bowl. I add a generous touch of grenadine to the water for color and put in some whole strawberries and woodruff sprigs to make it attractive. It does dilute the punch a bit, but by the time it melts, it usually doesn't matter.

Early spring flowers and foliage stay fresh in a wire wreath base filled with damp sphagnum moss around this traditional May wine bowl.

AN EDIBLE FLOWER GARDEN

LEGEND

1 – *Daylily*
2 – *Pineapple Sage*
3 – *Rose*
4 – *Bergamot*
5 – *Garlic Chives*
6 – *Anise Hyssop*
7 – *Sage*
8 – *Lavender*
9 – *Chives*
10 – *Borage*
11 – *Coriander*
12 – *Rocket*
13 – *Nasturtiums*
14 – *Dill*
15 – *Fennel*
16 – *Basil*
17 – *Opal Basil*
18 – *Gem Marigolds*
19 – *Calendula*
20 – *Rosemary*
21 – *Violets*
22 – *Marjoram*
23 – *Oregano*
24 – *Thyme*
25 – *Pinks*
26 – *Violas*

Your edible flower garden can be planted in nice straight rows, tucked into borders, or even set in tubs or pots on a patio or deck. Use your imagination to create a plan that suits your space and needs.

The fanciful viola-shaped garden shown here contains three perennial beds and two annual beds with little pathways between the "petals". The two perennial beds in the back contain the taller and larger plants. The left bed groups red and orange blooms with some white ones, while the right bed combines purple, lavender, and pink flowers. The two annual beds have taller plants in the rear and the smaller ones in the front. The front perennial bed contains the smaller, low-growing flowers and herbs.

Most of the flowers listed in this book grow best in full sun. Since sweet woodruff needs at least partial shade, and mint, which thrives in sun or partial shade, needs to be contained or placed in a spot where you don't mind its spreading, I haven't included them in this plan.

This plan will provide more than enough flowers to enjoy and share with friends. The sketch can easily be altered to suit your needs and preferences: if you can't stand the taste of calendulas and adore the flavor of basil, then substitute different types of basil for the calendulas.

Garden soil should be well drained and fertile. Add fertilizer or manure to enrich less-than-perfect soil, but avoid adding too much nitrogen, which might inhibit flower formation. Mulch makes a garden look tidy and finished. It also helps retain moisture so that less water is required and best of all, keeps the weeds to a minimum. Be vigilant about removing faded blooms to encourage your garden to produce more flowers.

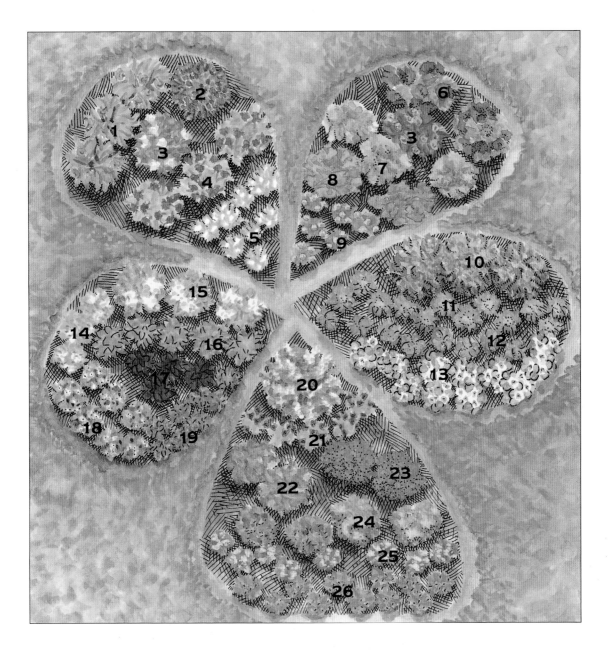

F I F T Y   E D I B L E   F L O W E R S

This chart contains 50 well-known flowers that are edible. It does not contain every edible flower; some don't taste good, and others that are considered edible aren't really safe to eat. The flowers listed here should appeal to just about everyone's taste buds.

You'll find common and botanical names and types, estimated height at maturity and space to allow between plants, color, flavor, and fragrance, and comments. (The term "cvs." following the botanical name of a plant means that it also includes its cultivars.)

The time of bloom listed is that in my Zone 7 garden in Maryland. These dates can vary by as much as several weeks, depending on where you live. Short-lived annuals like coriander prefer warm days and long nights. Grown under these conditions, they will complete their life cycle long before those that are grown in cool temperate zones. Whether you sow seed or put in established plants

Species	Plant type	Plant height (feet)	Plant spacing (feet)	Time of bloom
ANISE HYSSOP (*Agastache foeniculum*)	P	3–4	1–2	Jul–Sep
APPLE (*Malus* sp.)	P	8–30	20	May
BASIL (*Ocimum basilicum* cvs.)	A	1–3	1–2	Jul–frost
BERGAMOT (*Monarda didyma* cvs.)	P	3–4	1½	Jul
BORAGE (*Borago officinalis*)	A	2–2½	1–1½	Jun–Jul
BURNET (*Poterium sanguisorba*)	P	⅔–1	1	Jul
CALENDULA (*Calendula officinalis*)	A	1–2	½–1	Jun–Aug
CHERVIL (*Anthriscus cerefolium*)	A	1–1½	⅔–1	May–Jun
CHIVE (*Allium schoenoprasum*)	P	1½–2	⅔–1	May–Jun
CHIVE, GARLIC (*A. tuberosum*)	P	2–2½	⅔–1	Aug–Sep
CHRYSANTHEMUM, FLORIST'S (*Chrysanthemum x morifolium*)	P	2–2½	1–2	Sep–Oct
CHRYSANTHEMUM, GARLAND (*C. coronarium*)	P	3	2	Sep–Oct
CORIANDER (*Coriandrum sativum*)	A	2–3	½–1½	Jun–frost
DAISY, ENGLISH (*Bellis perennis*)	P	½	½	Apr–Sep
DAISY, OXEYE (*Chrysanthemum leucanthemum*)	P	1–3	½–1	Apr–Aug
DANDELION (*Taraxacum officinale*)	P	½	½–1	May–Jul
DAYLILY (*Hemerocallis fulva*)	P	2½–3½	1½–2½	Jun–Jul
DILL (*Anethum graveolens*)	A	3–5	½–1	Jun–frost
ELDERBERRY (*Sambucus caerulea. S. canadensis*)	P	5–12	5–12	May–Jun
FENNEL (*Foeniculum vulgare*)	P	3–6	1½–2	Jul–Aug
GLADIOLUS (*Gladiolus* sp.)	TP	1–3	½–1	6–8 wk from planting bulb
GRAPE HYACINTH (*Muscari atlanticum, M. botryoides*)	P	½–⅔	⅓–½	Apr–May
HOLLYHOCK (*Alcea rosea*)	B	4–9	1	Jul–Sep
HONEYSUCKLE (*Lonicera* sp.)	P	6–20		May–Jul
LAVENDER (*Lavandula angustifolia* cvs.)	P	1½–2	2–3	Jun–Jul
LEMON (*Citrus limon*)	P	8–20	12–16	Varies with variety

A: annual; B: biennial; P: perennial; TP: tender perennial

when the danger of frost is past will also affect flowering time. An established plant will flower weeks earlier than one sown from seed. Plants grown in greenhouses or on window sills or held over in cold frames will often bloom out of season.

Most herb flowers taste very similar to their leaves. Some are a bit milder with more perfume while others are stronger and a little bitter. Different varieties of roses can taste sweet and aromatic or downright sour and bitter. First smell, and then always taste a flower before you use it.

Note: Because a person, especially one who is prone to allergies, can have an allergic reaction to flowers, as to any food, proceed with caution when trying unfamiliar ones.

Color	Taste	Fragrance	Comments
Dusky I-V	Strong anise-licorice, sweet, tasty	—	Herb
PP	Slightly floral, sour	Sweet floral	Fruit tree; petals candy well.
W to PP	Spicy, sweet, like leaves but milder	—	Herb; sow continuously for harvest until frost.
R,P,W, V	Perfumy, tealike, like leaves but more aromatic, less herby	—	—
B-Pu, L	Slight cucumber	—	Mainly used as garnish; candies well
Raspberry	Strong green, hint of cucumber	—	Salad herb
Y,G,O	Slightly green, tangy, peppery	—	Ornamental; dries well
W	Parsleylike with hint of tarragon, citrus	—	Herb; winter in cold frame.
L,R-P	Onion, strong	—	Herb; separate into florets to serve.
W	Onion-garlic, strong	—	Herb; separate into florets to serve.
W,Y,O,R,P,Pu	Each var. different, some strong, bitter	Pungent	Ornamental
Y,Y-W	Milder than florist mums	—	Ornamental
W	Like leaf but more fragrant	—	Herb; sow continuously for several harvests.
W,P; Y center	Mild	—	Eat raw in salad or use as garnish.
W; Y center	Mild	—	Eat raw in salad or use as garnish.
Y	Like leaves: bitter	—	Eat cooked or infused.
TO	Cooked, like asparagus/zucchini cross	—	All parts of plant are edible.
Y	Like leaves but more intense	—	Sow continuously for harvest until frost.
C	Mild floral	—	Other spp. of *Sambucus* are poisonous.
PY	Licorice, milder than leaves, sweet	—	—
Various except TB	Mediocre	—	Best as container or garnish
P-B	Grapey, slightly sour, with bitter aftertaste	Grapey	—
Various except TB	Little, slightly bitter	—	Best as container or garnish
C,Y,P	Sweet honey perfumy	Sweet, floral	Invasive habit
L,Pu,P,W	Highly perfumed	Clean, fresh	Taste, may be very strong; some vars. will rebloom.
W	Citrus, slightly bitter; some vars. sweeter; highly perfumed	Sweet, floral	Subtropical tree

COLOR: B, blue; C, creamy white; DB, dark blue; G, gold; I, indigo; L, lavender; Li, lilac; M, mahogany; O, orange; P, pink; PB, pale blue; PP, pale pink; PPu, pale purple; Pu, purple; PY, pale yellow; R, red; TB, true blue; TO, tawny orange; V, violet; W, white; Y, yellow.

Species	Plant type	Plant height (feet)	Plant spacing (feet)	Time of bloom
LEMON BALM (*Melissa officinalis*)	P	1½–2	1½–2	Jul–Aug
LILAC (*Syringa vulgaris*)	P	6–15	6	Apr–May
LOVAGE (*Levisticum officinale*)	B	4–6	2–3	Aug
MARIGOLD, AFRICAN (*Tagetes erecta*)	A	1½–3	2–3	May–Sep
MARIGOLD, SIGNET (*T. tenuifolia*)	A	1–2	1–2	May–Sep
MARJORAM (*Origanum majorana*)	TP	1	1	Jun–Aug
OREGANO (*Origanum* sp.)	P	1–1½	1–1½	Jun–Aug
MINT (*Mentha* sp.)	P	2–3	1–2	Jul–Sep
MUSTARD (*Brassica* sp.)	A	1–2	½	Apr–May
NASTURTIUM (*Tropaeolum majus*)	A	1–1½	1–1½	Jul–Aug
ORANGE (*Citrus sinensis*)	P	12–40	20	Varies with variety
PEA, GARDEN (*Pisum sativum*)	A	1	½–⅔	May–Jun
PINK (*Dianthus* sp.)	P	½–1	1	Jun–Jul
PLUM (*Prunus* sp.)	P	8–15	20	Apr–May
RED CLOVER (*Trifolium pratense*)	P	1–2	½	Jun–Sep
ROCKET (*Eruca vesicaria*)	A	1½–2	½–⅔	May–frost
ROSE (*Rosa* sp.)	P	6–20	⅔–6	May–Jun, Sep
ROSEMARY (*Rosmarinus officinalis* cvs.)	TP	2–6	3–8	Depends on variety
SAGE, GARDEN (*Salvia officinalis* cvs.)	P	1½–2½	1½–2½	May–Jul
SAGE, PINEAPPLE (*S. elegans*)	TP	3–4½	2–3	Sep
SAVORY, SUMMER (*Satureja hortensis*)	A	⅔–1½	⅔–1	Jul–Aug
SAVORY, WINTER (*S. montana*)	P	2–1	1–2	Jul–Aug
SCARLET RUNNER BEAN (*Phaseolus coccineus*)	TP	4–5	½–⅔	Jul–Aug
SCENTED GERANIUM (*Pelargonium* sp.)	TP	1–3	1–3	Sporadically throughout year
SQUASH (*Cucurbita* sp.)	A	2–3	3–4	Jul–Aug
SWEET WOODRUFF (*Galium odoratum*)	P	½–1	½–1	May
THYME (*Thymus* sp.)	P	½–1	1–1½	Jul–Aug
TULIP (*Tulipa* sp.)	P	½–2½	½–⅚	Apr–May
VIOLET; PANSY; JOHNNY-JUMP-UP (*Viola odorata*; *V.* x *wittrockiana*, *V. tricolor*)	P,A,A	½–1	½–1	Apr–May;May–Jul
YUCCA (*Yucca filamentosa*)	P	3–6	2–3	Jul

A: annual; B: biennial; P: perennial; TP: tender perennial

Color	Taste	Fragrance	Comments
C	Very sweet, lemony	—	Herb
W to P-Pu,Li	Very perfumy, slightly bitter	—	Candies well
Y-W	Mild celery	—	Herb
W,Y,G,O,R,M	Variable; some cultivars less intense and bitter	Strong, pungent	Ornamental
W,Y,G,O,R,M	Gem cvs. citrusy and milder than *T. erecta*	—	Ornamental
PP	Like leaves; spicy, sweet	—	Herb
W	Like leaves; spicy, pungent	—	Herb
L,P,W	Minty; milder than leaves	—	Herb
Y	Mustardy, hot	—	Use as zesty salad garnish.
	Piquant, like watercress	—	Good as container and in salads
W	Highly perfumed, citrus, strongly orangy like skin	Sweet, strong	Subtropical tree
W tinged P	Raw peas	—	Vegetable
P,W,R	Little flavor, like mild salad herb; clove and cottage pinks spicier, like cloves	Some varieties spicy/sweet	Ornamental
P-W	Mild, like flower nectar	Pleasingly sweet	Tree petals candy well.
P,L	Hay, green	Hay	A forage plant; scatter florets on salad.
W, R-P veins	Like leaves, less piquant, nutty, smoky	—	Salad green; sow continuously for harvest until frost.
W,Y,O,R,P	Highly perfumed, sweet to bitter	—	Ornamental; remove sour white petal base
PB,DB,P,W	Mild rosemary; slightly resinous but more flowery, delicate	—	Herb; don't cook.
B-Pu,W,P	Flowery sage, slightly musky	—	Herb
Scarlet	Flowery pineapple, hint of sage muskiness	—	Herb
P	Mildly peppery and herby, sweet	—	Herb
PB-Pu	Mildly peppery and herby, spicy	—	Herb
Bright O-scarlet	Like raw bean but milder	—	Vegetable; flower crunchy, good raw in salad
W,P,R,Pu	Like var. (lemon, rose, etc.); may be slightly sour or bitter	Mild, pleasing	Ornamental
O-Y	Vegetably, mildly of raw squash	Slightly floral	Vegetable
W	Sweet, grassy, vanilla	Sweet hay with hint of vanilla	Herb, ornamental ground cover
PPu,W	Like leaves but milder	—	Herb; most creeping thymes have little flavor
Various except TB	Little; slightly sweet or bitter	—	Best as container or garnish
V,P,W;V,W,Pi,Y	Mild like a leafy green except *V. odorata*, which is sweet	*V. odorata:* sweet	Ornamental
C with Pu tinge	Vegetably, slightly bitter with hint of artichoke	—	Ornamental or forage

COLOR: B, blue; C, creamy white; DB, dark blue; G, gold; I, indigo; L, lavender; Li, lilac; M, mahogany; O, orange; P, pink; PB, pale blue; PP, pale pink; PPu, pale purple; Pu, purple; PY, pale yellow; R, red; TB, true blue; TO, tawny orange; V, violet; W, white; Y, yellow.

ANISE HYSSOP

Agastache foeniculum

This handsome perennial stands erect and usually reaches about 3 to 4 feet in height. It prefers sun, but can stand some shade, and likes well-drained, fertile soil. From June to September, it is covered with 2-inch-long spikes of tiny two-lipped flowers that might be pinkish mauve or dusky violet. Anise hyssop is easily grown from seed, and mature plants will provide plenty of volunteers to extend your planting or share with friends.

Its leaves and tiny flowers smell and taste of anise, but the square stems and opposite leaves of anise hyssop tell you it belongs to a different family entirely, the Lamiaceae or mint family. The leaves look a bit like those of catnip, another mint-family member, but larger.

The flowers of anise hyssop have the good, sweet flavor of anise or licorice, with a slight floral perfume. They're delicious nibbled right off the plant, and they work especially well in baked goods and desserts. Try them in a cup of hot tea for an interesting extra flavor, or as a garnish for cold drinks, soups, and salads.

Each tiny anise hyssop corolla can be removed from its calyx for a delicate taste, or the entire florets can be stripped from the stem for a larger yield and a stronger flavor.

ANISE HYSSOP AND ALMOND BUTTER COOKIES

Anise is a traditional flavoring for butter cookies; using anise hyssop blossoms in place of an extract results in a delicate whisper of flavor.

MAKES FIVE TO SIX DOZEN COOKIES

1 cup sugar

1/4 cup anise hyssop florets
  removed from their stems

1 extra-large egg

12 tablespoons unsalted butter,
  cut into 12 pieces

1/2 teaspoon vanilla extract

2 cups unbleached flour

Scant 1/2 teaspoon salt

3 ounces almonds, lightly
  toasted and coarsely chopped

Combine the sugar and the anise hyssop flowers in a food processor and pulse until blended.

Add the egg and process for about 60 seconds. Add the butter and vanilla and process for another 60 seconds.

Mix the flour and salt and add it to the processor. Process for about 20 seconds, until most of the flour has been incorporated. Add the almonds and process until just mixed; do not overprocess.

Turn the dough out onto a lightly floured surface and gather it into a ball. Divide it into three parts and roll each in plastic wrap into a cylinder 1 1/2 to 2 inches in diameter. Chill for about 1 hour, until firm, or place in the freezer for about 20 minutes.

Preheat the oven to 350° F. Slice the dough slightly less than 1/4 inch thick with a sharp knife. Place the rounds at least 1/2 inch apart on ungreased baking sheets.

Bake for about 12 minutes, changing the position of the baking sheets halfway through baking, until the edges of the cookies are just golden brown. Remove from baking sheets immediately to cool on racks. When cool, store in airtight containers.

O c i m u m   b a s i l i c u m

There are many wonderful flavored basils—anise, cinnamon, lemon, opal, and spice are just a few—but my favorite, for its robust, spicy flavor, is the Italian Genoa Green. Basil blooms vary in flavor according to variety as the foliage does, but all taste of cloves with a hint of citrus and mint.

The best way to remove the florets from the basil plant is to snip the stem closely above and below each flower whorl, discarding the stems in between which are sometimes bitter.

Basil is a companion plant to tomatoes in the garden and the kitchen, and it is the main ingredient of the classic pesto. It is good with all the summer vegetables: corn, eggplant, peppers, squash, and tomatoes. Cheese dishes, fish, and fowl can be flavored with basil, as can butters, vinegars, and oils. Any salad is improved by basil's presence. The scented basils add interesting flavors to fruits and desserts. Try basil flowers in any recipe where you would use fresh snipped leaves.

Native to India and used in the Mediterranean for thousands of years, this aromatic annual must have hot, full sun to thrive. Different varieties may reach 1 to 3 feet in height. The small flowers, which range in color from white to pink to pale lavender, are borne with a few small leaves in

whorls along stems held above the leaves. For earliest harvest, start basil seedlings indoors in strong light 6 to 8 weeks before last frost date.

Tomato and Cucumber Salad with Basil Flowers

This dish is a great appetizer accompanied by a glass of wine and a crusty loaf of bread. Or better yet, make it lunch with a bowl of olives and some sardines. It is best made with fresh imported mozzarella, but a domestic mozzarella will do.

Serves Six to Eight

2 medium ripe tomatoes

1 medium cucumber

1 medium sweet onion such as Vidalia, Walla Walla, or Texas

8 ounces mozzarella cheese

About 3 tablespoons olive oil

Salt and freshly ground pepper

1/3 cup basil flowers (cut the flower stems in between each whorl as described on page 33)

Core and chop the tomatoes into 3/4-inch dice. Peel the cucumber, quarter it lengthwise, and then cut it into 1/2-inch pieces. Cut the onion into 1/2-inch dice. Combine all the vegetables in a bowl.

Cut the cheese into 1/2-inch dice, or if using fresh mozzarella, shred it into bite-sized pieces. Add the cheese to the vegetables and toss.

Drizzle the oil over the vegetable mixture and season with salt and pepper. Toss the vegetables with the basil flowers and taste for seasoning. Add a bit more olive oil if the salad is not moist enough. Let the salad marinate at least 30 minutes, and as long as a few hours, before serving. Refrigerate it in hot weather, allowing it to come to cool room temperature for serving.

BERGAMOT

Monarda didyma

Bergamot grows from 2 to 4 feet tall in sun or partial shade, and is happiest in moist soil or mulch. The shaggy flower heads stand above the leaves, sometimes with a second flower head appearing to grow out of the center of the first. Scarlet is the most common and best-known color form of this species, but cultivars extend the color range from white and coral to pink and lavender.

Bees as well as hummingbirds are attracted to the nectar of this strongly aromatic perennial herb, known also as bee balm. Another name, Oswego tea, refers to its use as a beverage by Indians from the Oswego River area in New York near Lake Ontario.

Bergamot may owe its name to the resemblance of its fragrance to that of the bergamot orange. However, it is the latter, *not* the herb bergamot, whose oil is a component of Earl Grey tea and some perfumes. The flavor of the blooms is strong and flowery, almost tea-like, with citrus undertones. The flowers with the most perfume have the strongest flavor. To use them in the kitchen, rinse the flower heads gently and pat dry. Pull the individual florets from the blossom head.

Bergamot flowers are great with fruit, especially summer fruits such as apricots, peaches, and plums. They are delicious in jams and jellies, baked goods, custards, and desserts, and make a colorful garnish for beverages and salads.

PEACH SHORTCAKES WITH BERGAMOT FLOWERS

Bergamot flowers add a special sweetness and colorful accent to this classic all-American dessert.

EIGHT THREE-INCH SHORTCAKES

6 to 8 very ripe peaches, peeled and sliced

1 tablespoon lemon juice

1 to 2 tablespoons sugar

2 to 3 tablespoons bergamot flowers

2 cups unbleached white flour

1 tablespoon baking powder

Scant 1/2 teaspoon salt

3 tablespoons sugar

6 tablespoons unsalted butter

1 cup half-and-half with 1 tablespoon bergamot flowers

1 tablespoon unsalted butter, melted

Whipping cream or vanilla ice cream

Preheat oven to 425° F and lightly butter a baking sheet.

Toss the peaches in a bowl with the lemon juice, sugar, and half of the bergamot flowers. If the fruit is tart, use the larger amount of sugar; if it is sweet, use less. Reserve the remaining flowers for garnishing the dessert.

Combine the flour, baking powder, salt, and 2 tablespoons of the sugar in a bowl or food processor. Cut the butter into the mixture until it is a coarse meal. Add the half-and-half with the bergamot flowers to the dry ingredients and mix until just blended; do not overmix.

Turn the dough onto a floured surface and knead 8 or 10 times. Roll or pat the dough to about 3/4 inch thick. Using a 3-inch cutter, cut out rounds, using all of the dough.

Place the rounds of dough on the baking sheet, brush the tops with the melted butter, and sprinkle them with the reserved tablespoon of sugar.

Bake the cakes in the center of the oven for 12 to 14 minutes, or until golden brown. Cool the shortcakes for at least 5 minutes before splitting them open; they are best served warm, but are good at room temperature.

To assemble the shortcakes, split them in half. Place a spoonful of fruit on the bottom half with a bit of the juice. Add a dollop of whipped cream or a spoonful of ice cream and cover with the top half of the shortcake. Repeat layers of fruit and cream and garnish the top with a few peach slices. Scatter the reserved bergamot blossoms over the desserts and serve immediately.

BORAGE

Borago officinalis

The star-shaped flowers that adorn the pale green, hairy foliage are most commonly bright blue, but occasionally may be pink or lavender. These are some of the prettiest little edible flowers, and they hold up quite well after picking.

To prepare the flowers, gently pull each blossom by its black center to release it from its hairy calyx. Gently rinse and pat dry. Keep flowers in the refrigerator between damp paper towels if not using them right away.

Borage flowers have much the same cucumbery flavor as the leaves. I like to use them with cucumbers to echo that taste. They are a handsome, sturdy garnish for dips, salads, and beverages. Traditionally, borage flowers have been most often used to adorn wine cups and teas. Float them in punch bowls or use them to garnish a simple glass of iced tea or lemonade. They are pretty frozen in ice cubes, and perfect for candying.

Borage is a hardy annual that prefers full sun and grows about 2¹/₂ feet tall. It has a tendency to sprawl and take up a lot of space; sometimes it gets so heavy it falls over. You can stake it for a tidier look if you like. Once you have a borage plant, most likely you'll have volunteer seedlings for years to come.

HERBED CUCUMBER DIP WITH BORAGE BLOSSOMS

This dip can be served with crackers or chips, or with fresh vegetable crudités such as carrots, cucumbers, jerusalem artichokes, celery, or bell peppers. It is also good as a condiment with baked or grilled fish or slices of steamed new potato.

MAKES A GENEROUS THREE CUPS

1 medium cucumber, peeled and seeded

1 scant teaspoon white wine vinegar

1/2 teaspoon soy sauce

3 dashes Angostura bitters

Pinch sugar

Salt and freshly ground white pepper

1 garlic clove, pressed

2 teaspoons finely chopped parsley

2 teaspoons finely chopped basil

1 tablespoon finely chopped dill

1⅓ cups sour cream

2/3 cup yogurt

About 20 borage blossoms

Finely chop the cucumber. In a mixing bowl, combine the cucumber with the vinegar, soy sauce, bitters, and sugar, and season with salt and freshly ground pepper. Blend well and let stand while preparing the garlic and herbs. Add the garlic and herbs, toss well, and add the sour cream and yogurt. Combine well, cover, and chill for at least 30 minutes before serving.

The dip can be made several hours ahead. Transfer it to a pretty bowl and garnish with a circle of borage blossoms just before serving.

CALENDULA

Calendula officinalis

The edible part of the calendula blossom is the "petal" (actually the ray flower), as the center of the flower (which comprises the disk flowers) is strong and bitter. To remove petals, grasp the bloom in one hand and gently pull the petals from the disk.

Calendulas have long been used to color butters and cheeses. They seem to add more color than flavor to most dishes. The taste vaguely suggests marigolds: herbaceous and slightly musky. Calendula petals are most commonly used cooked in rice dishes, custards, and puddings, but they are also good added to baked goods and egg dishes, and as a garnish for salads and vegetables.

The petals can be dried for use in winter soups and stews. They are best dried on paper rather than screens or baskets, as they have a tendency to stick to the surface that they're dried on.

The calendula, or pot marigold, is a hardy annual that frequently self-sows. It likes full sun, though it can tolerate some shade, and it stands anywhere from 6 to 18

inches tall. The pale green leaves are set off by daisylike blooms in shades of yellow, gold, and orange. Some newer varieties have double or fringed blossoms.

GOLDEN CORN MUFFINS WITH CALENDULA PETALS

Calendula petals add a bright color accent to these hearty, wholesome muffins.

MAKES ONE DOZEN LARGE MUFFINS

1 cup stone-ground cornmeal

3/4 cup unbleached white flour

2 teaspoons baking powder

1/2 teaspoon salt

2 extra-large eggs

1 cup milk

3 tablespoons corn or vegetable oil

3/4 cup grated cheddar cheese

1 cup corn kernels, fresh, or frozen and thawed

1/4 cup calendula petals

Butter a muffin tin and preheat the oven to 375° F. In a mixing bowl combine the cornmeal, flour, baking powder, and salt. In another bowl, beat the eggs and add the milk and oil, blending well. Stir the cheese and corn into the wet ingredients.

Pour the wet ingredients into the dry and blend. Stir the calendula petals into the batter. Fill the muffin tins almost full, dividing the batter evenly.

Bake for 20 minutes or until golden brown. Let stand for 5 minutes, remove the muffins from the tin, and serve warm with or without butter or molasses.

CHIVES

Allium schoenoprasum and A. tuberosum

Common chive and garlic chive are hardy perennials of the onion family. The common chive may grow 2 feet tall and blooms in midspring. Its dense spherical flower umbels are a lovely reddish purple. The garlic chive plant can reach 2¹/₂ feet in height and is covered in late summer

To prepare the flower head of the common chive, hold it in one hand with the stem facing out. With a sharp pair of scissors, make two cuts in a V, cutting deep inside the blossom on either side of the stem, so that the individual florets fall away from the stem. Handle the garlic chive blooms in the same manner, but snip straight across the individual flower stems just below the florets.

The flowers taste much like the leaves; the flavor seems a bit hot to the palate at first, but then a nice oniony aroma lingers. The flavor of the garlic chive flower is a bit more pungent than that of the common chive.

Chive flowers flavor butters, vinegars, sauces, soups, and vegetables. They are good with cheese and egg dishes, potatoes, and tomatoes. Use them to garnish many foods, from salads to grilled meats. For a special treat, dip the whole blossoms in a tempura batter and fry them.

with pure white blooms borne in umbels. Both are attractive in the perennial border as well as in the herb garden; the dried seed heads of garlic chives are striking in the winter garden.

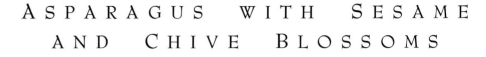

ASPARAGUS WITH SESAME AND CHIVE BLOSSOMS

Bright lavender chive blossoms begin to bloom in my garden about the time the asparagus bed is at its peak. Hence, we have a natural combination and a simple tasty dish. Since chive blossoms are so strong in flavor, I add them at the last minute in this recipe.

SERVES FOUR TO SIX

1 pound asparagus, washed, trimmed, and cut diagonally into 1-inch lengths

1 tablespoon olive oil

1 tablespoon sesame seed

2 tablespoons fresh snipped chives

About 16 chive blossoms, stems removed to separate flowers

About 1/2 teaspoon soy sauce

Salt and freshly ground pepper to taste

A few whole chive blossoms for garnish

Blanch the asparagus in lightly salted boiling water for about 3 minutes or until crisp-tender; do not overcook. Refresh under cold water and drain well.

In a skillet, heat the oil over medium heat and add the sesame seed. Stir for 1 minute, add the snipped chives, and stir for 1 minute more.

Add the asparagus and soy sauce to the skillet with a few pinches of salt and generous grindings of pepper; stir well, cover, and cook for a minute or so.

Remove the lid, sprinkle the chive blooms over the asparagus, and cover for 1 to 2 minutes so that the chive blooms steam briefly.

Stir lightly and taste for seasoning. Serve hot. Garnish each plate with a whole blossom or the serving dish with a few.

DAYLILY

Hemerocallis fulva

The orange blossoms of this very hardy perennial are found in gardens as well as along roadsides. Related species have yellow and deep orange-bronze flowers. The plants, which grow 2 to 4 feet tall, have bright green swordlike leaves. They thrive in full sun or partial shade; those grown in heavy shade have fewer flowers. Plants are free and vigorous, increasing rapidly by rhizomes.

All parts of the daylily are edible. Smaller buds, about 2 inches long or less, are best for eating; bigger ones tend to be bitter. Petals can be pulled from the flower and used whole or cut into a finely shredded chiffonade.

You'll need to sample the flowers you plan to use, as flavors vary depending upon where and how the plants are grown: from a mild vegetable taste that is slightly floral to acid, bitter, or even metallic flavors.

When sautéd, braised, or stir-fried, the buds taste like a delicate cross between asparagus and zucchini; they are good with pasta, vegetables, poultry, and meat. Use the petals to garnish salads, or add them to soups or vegetables. Petals and buds are often dried and added to Oriental dishes, especially rice, soups, and stir-fries.

PASTA WITH DAYLILY BUDS AND MUSHROOMS

I like to serve this pasta dish garnished with homemade croutons made from one or two slices of bread torn into small pieces and sautéed in a little butter until they are crispy and golden brown.

SERVES FOUR

About 6 ounces oyster or shiitake mushrooms

1 heaping cup daylily buds, 1 1/2 to 2 inches long

2 tablespoons unsalted butter

2 tablespoons olive oil

2 shallots, finely minced

1/2 teaspoon fresh chopped marjoram

1 tablespoon fresh chopped Italian parsley

Salt and freshly ground pepper

Freshly grated parmesan

1 pound fresh fettuccine noodles

Put the pasta water on to boil while preparing the vegetables.

Clean the mushrooms with a brush or a damp paper towel; do not rinse. Tear them into large, bite-sized pieces; remove the tough stems of shiitakes. Rinse the daylily buds and pat them dry.

In a large skillet, heat the butter and oil over medium heat. Add the shallots and sauté them for about a minute. Add the mushrooms and stir for a minute or two. Add the daylily buds and stir for 2 to 3 minutes more.

Add the herbs and season with salt and pepper. Cover the skillet and let it stand over very low heat for a few minutes while the pasta cooks. Drain the pasta, add it to the pan of vegetables, and toss well. Add another tablespoon of butter or olive oil if necessary. Taste for seasoning and serve hot. Garnish with breadcrumbs if desired, and pass the parmesan.

FENNEL

Foeniculum vulgare

Fennel flowers taste like the rest of the plant, like mild licorice but with a sweet perfume. Scatter them over salads, vegetables, or seafood. They taste best with artichokes, potatoes, tomatoes, beets, and fish, and give a mild, pleasing flavor to tomato and cream sauces and vinaigrettes.

The easiest way to harvest the flowers is to cut the entire umbel from the stalk and bring it into the kitchen. Rinse the flowers and keep the whole stalk in a glass of water until ready to use. To separate the florets, snip the individual stems right below the flowers.

The herb fennel is a perennial that is usually grown as an annual in colder regions. However, for a fast start each season, the plants can be dug in the fall, trimmed back leaving a few inches of stem, wintered over in a cold frame or root cellar, and replanted in spring. Fennel plants can grow to be 4 to 6 feet tall and bear large umbels of yellow flowers. The attractive bronze-leaved fennel (F. v. var. dulce cv.) also bears yellow edible flowers. (Florence fennel, F. v. var. azoricum, is grown chiefly for its thickened leaf bases.)

ARTICHOKE AND POTATO SALAD WITH FENNEL FLOWERS

The complementary flavors of fennel and artichokes elevate a humble potato salad to new heights.

SERVES THREE TO FOUR

2 large artichokes

1 pound new potatoes

1 small onion

1/2 large yellow bell pepper, roasted, seeded, and peeled

About 1/4 cup olive oil

3 or 4 umbels of fennel flowers with stalks about 6 to 8 inches long

Juice of half a lemon

Salt and freshly ground black pepper

Remove leaves, stems, and chokes from the artichokes and trim away the tough parts. Put the artichoke hearts in water to which you've added a tablespoon of lemon juice.

Scrub the potatoes, cut into 3/4 inch dice, and steam until just tender. Transfer them to a bowl to cool.

While the potatoes are cooking, cut the onion into quarters lengthwise and slice it crosswise into 1/4-inch slices. Soak the onion in cold water. Cut the pepper into strips lengthwise and cut the strips into 1-inch lengths.

Pat the artichoke hearts dry and cut them in half across. Slice the halves crosswise in 1/4-inch slices. In a small skillet, heat 1 tablespoon of the olive oil over medium heat. Sauté the artichokes, stirring occasionally, for about 5 to 6 minutes, until crisp-tender.

Slice two of the fennel stalks very thinly, and put them in a small bowl. Snip the flowers into another small bowl and reserve them for garnish. Add the remaining olive oil and lemon juice to the bowl containing the sliced fennel stalks. Season generously with salt and freshly ground pepper and blend well with a fork.

Pour this dressing over the warm potatoes and toss well. Squeeze the onion dry and add it to the potatoes with the sautéed artichokes and peppers. Toss the salad well, taste, and adjust seasoning.

Serve the salad in a shallow bowl, perhaps on a bed of greens, warm or at room temperature. Scatter the fennel flowers over the top.

LAVENDER

Lavandula angustifolia

This shrubby perennial with gray-green foliage and spikes of tiny lavender flowers is famous for its perfume. Plants grow to about 2 feet tall in full sun. Cultivars of this species have flower spikes that vary in length from less than 1 inch to 3 inches long and range in color from deep violet to the traditional lavender to white and pink. Some of the newer hybrids will rebloom 60 days after their first flowering.

Lavender blooms are highly aromatic and taste much like they smell: perfumy, vaguely oily, with the heavy muskiness of lavender and a hint of lemon. Generally, the varieties with darker flower buds are more attractive and flavorful for use in the kitchen.

To remove lavender flowers from stems, grasp the stem in one hand and strip off the flowers with the forefinger and thumb of the other hand.

Use lavender blossoms sparingly in desserts—ice creams, custards, puddings, and with fruit. Lavender goes well with all sorts of berries, too. It also makes for interesting jellies and vinegars. The famous dried herb blend Herbes de Provence contains a mixture of lavender blossoms, thyme, savory, basil, and fennel, and is suggested for use with all types of meat and fish, as well as in sauces and on pizza.

RASPBERRIES WITH LAVENDER CREAM

I originally envisioned this creamy custard with red raspberries. After trying it with other berries, I found it to be quite tasty with black raspberries and blackberries, and better yet, blueberries. A mélange of berries will have your taste buds tap-dancing. Lavender blooms are very fragrant; the cream is full-flavored, and a little goes a long way.

SERVES EIGHT

1/2 cup whipping cream

1/2 cup milk

2 tablespoons light honey (wildflower or lavender honey is good)

3 tablespoons sugar

Pinch salt

5 lavender spikes, 2¹/₂ to 3 inches long

2 extra-large egg yolks

1/2 cup whipping cream, stiffly whipped

About 2 pints fresh berries, picked over, then rinsed just before serving

In a double boiler over very hot water, combine the cream, milk, honey, sugar, salt, and lavender blossoms. Cook over simmering water for 10 minutes, stirring occasionally.

Beat the yolks in a small bowl. Pour about 1/2 cup of the lavender cream mixture over the yolks and whisk well. Return the cream and yolk mixture to the double boiler and mix well. Cook over just-simmering water for 10 minutes, stirring, until the mixture thickens. Remove from heat and strain the custard cream through a sieve into a stainless steel bowl. Discard the lavender.

Let the custard cream cool to room temperature with a piece of waxed paper covering the bowl, then chill. Or to cool it more quickly, place the bowl of custard cream in a larger bowl filled with ice, and stir occasionally until cooled, then chill. The cream will thicken a bit as it cools.

Remove the lavender cream from the refrigerator 10 or 15 minutes before serving. Fold in the freshly whipped cream. Spoon a little lavender cream onto each dessert plate and arrange the berries on top. Serve immediately.

MARIGOLD

Tagetes species

All marigold blossoms are edible, though some varieties are far more palatable than others. Most of the commonly grown, big African beauties are among the "others". The small-flowered signet marigolds (*T. tenuifolia*, "Pumila" group), are best for eating. 'Tangerine Gem' and 'Lemon Gem' belong to this group; they have a citrus perfume and flavor, as their names suggest, and less of the strong marigold aroma.

The blooms are small and can be used whole in salads, as a garnish, or dried for cooking. As the center of the flower tends to be bitter, especially in the larger marigolds, for best flavor pull off and use only the "petals" (botanically the ray flowers).

T. lucida is a tender perennial from Mexico that has an anise-licorice flavor. Its orange blooms can be used as a garnish or in soups, sauces, and salsas. *T. minuta* is an annual Peruvian marigold that grows to 9 or 10 feet tall. Both the bright yellow-orange flowers and the foliage are used as pungent flavoring for soups and stews, sauces, and especially salsas.

Look for marigolds with a milder flavor. Use the fresh petals in all kinds of salads or cook them in puddings, custards, and sauces or scrambled in eggs. In many old recipes, they were used to color and flavor rice dishes, cheeses, soups, stews, wines, sweet breads and rolls.

This popular annual is easy to grow from seed, transplants easily, and will grow in sun or part shade. It does well under almost

any conditions including acidic or poor soil. Mulching and fertilizing will provide you with prize-winning blooms. Marigolds will bloom all summer if you keep them deadheaded.

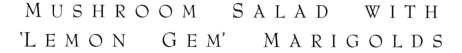

MUSHROOM SALAD WITH 'LEMON GEM' MARIGOLDS

The slight bitterness and hint of citrus of the marigold blossoms enhances the earthiness of mushrooms in this hearty salad.

SERVES SIX

3 cups thinly sliced mushrooms

About 3 cups tender baby lettuce leaves

About 1 cup chicory leaves

2 tablespoons fresh snipped chives

1/4 cup fresh dill sprigs

Handful of 'Lemon Gem' marigold blossoms

Small handful chive blossoms

Mayonnaise

Zest of 1 lemon

Handful 'Lemon Gem' marigold petals

1 clove garlic

1 extra-large egg yolk

3/4 cup olive oil

1 to 2 tablespoons lemon juice

Salt and freshly ground pepper

Do not wash the mushrooms; if they are dirty, brush them with a mushroom brush or a slightly dampened paper towel before slicing them. Wash the salad greens and spin or pat them dry. Rinse the herbs and flowers if necessary and pat them dry. Keep the salad ingredients cool until ready to assemble.

Lemon Mayonnaise

This mayonnaise can easily be prepared in a blender, but it tends to have a creamier texture when prepared by hand.

Put the lemon zest, marigold petals, and garlic in a mortar and bruise them well. Stir in the egg yolk. Add the oil, drop by drop, until the mixture begins to thicken; then in a fine stream, until the mayonnaise emulsifies. Stir in the lesser amount of lemon juice and season with salt and pepper. The mayonnaise should be a bit tart. Taste for seasoning.

Toss the mushrooms lightly with about one-third of the mayonnaise; add a little more mayonnaise if they are not moistened enough. Arrange the greens on a chilled platter. Scatter the chives and dill over the greens. Arrange the mushrooms on the salad. Scatter the marigolds and chive blossoms over the salad. Pass the remaining mayonnaise as the salad is served.

Variation using 'Tangerine Gem' marigolds: Prepare the salad as above but use golden beets, cooked until crisp tender, in place of the mushrooms, 'Tangerine Gem' marigolds, and orange zest and juice in place of lemon.

MARJORAM & OREGANO

Origanum majorana and O. vulgare

Sweet marjoram is a tender perennial herb and needs to be brought indoors where winters are cold, while oregano is a hardy perennial. Both plants like full sun, good drainage, and weed-free soil. Marjoram is the smaller of the two, growing about a foot tall; its flowers range from white to pink to pale purple. Oregano gets leggier and can reach 1½ feet in height; it usually has white blooms.

Marjoram and oregano are listed together as they both belong to the genus *Origanum*, and their flowers taste similar and can be used interchangeably. The flowers of both herbs, like their leaves, are spicy with a sweet perfume. However, marjoram flowers are milder, sweeter, and less pungent, while oregano flowers are heavier tasting, hot, and spicier. These flowers are compatible with all sorts of food—vegetables, cheeses, meat and poultry. They are a delicious garnish for salads, pizza, pasta, and Italian-style dishes.

To use the flowers in the kitchen, rinse them and pat dry. Pull or snip the individual florets from the stems. They can be coarsely chopped, if desired.

PIZZA WITH SUN-DRIED TOMATOES, GOAT CHEESE, AND MARJORAM OR OREGANO FLOWERS

MAKES TWO NINE- OR TEN-INCH PIZZAS

1 tablespoon active dry yeast

Pinch of sugar

1/4 cup warm water

2 cups unbleached white flour

1/4 cup rye flour

2/3 cup warm water

1 tablespoon olive oil

1/2 teaspoon salt

1 large clove garlic, very finely minced

1 1/2 tablespoons olive oil

Salt

3/4 cup oil-packed, sun-dried tomatoes, cut into 1/4-inch slivers

1 medium onion, quartered lengthwise and sliced thinly

5 1/2 ounces goat cheese, crumbled

1 tablespoon finely chopped Italian parsley

2 tablespoons marjoram or oregano blossoms

Olive oil for burnishing

To make the dough, dissolve the yeast and sugar in the 1/4 cup warm water. Mix the flours in a bowl and make a well in the center. When the yeast is foamy, add it to the well. Let the sponge rise about 5 minutes.

Gradually stir in the 2/3 cup water, adding 1 tablespoon olive oil and 1/2 teaspoon salt after half the water has been added. Stir well with a wooden spoon; the dough will be a bit sticky though very lively.

Turn the dough onto a floured surface and knead for 10 minutes, adding a little more flour if necessary. Transfer the dough to a lightly oiled bowl, cover with a damp tea towel, and let rise for 1 to 1 1/2 hours, until doubled in bulk. (Or cover the dough with plastic wrap and refrigerate it overnight; allow it to come to room temperature before proceeding.) Punch the dough down and let it rest for 15 minutes before forming into pizza shapes.

Prepare the pizza toppings; mix the minced garlic and olive oil. Preheat a baker's tile or pizza stone for 20 to 30 minutes in an oven set at 500° F.

Divide the pizza dough into two equal parts. Form one piece of dough into a 9- or 10-inch round on a pizza paddle that has been lightly dusted with flour or cornmeal to keep the pizza from sticking. Brush the top of the dough with half of the garlic in olive oil. Sprinkle lightly with salt. Spread half of the sun-dried tomatoes over the dough, and cover them with half of the onions.

Slide the pizza onto the baking stone and bake for about 5 minutes, until the crust is puffed around the edge and just starting to turn golden. Remove the pizza, using the paddle, and evenly spread half of the crumbled goat cheese over it. Return the pizza to the oven for about 3 minutes more, until the cheese begins to melt and the bottom crust is done.

Remove the pizza to a cutting board, sprinkle it with half of the herbs or flowers. Brush the edges lightly with olive oil. Repeat for the other pizza.

MINTS

Mentha species

The flavor of mint is unmistakable and assertive, yet it has a wide variety of affinities in the kitchen. Mint with lamb, with lemon, and with chocolate are all classic combinations, and only hint at the range of this hardy herb.

Mints are hardy perennial herbs found growing throughout the world from moist, shady spots to deserts. There is an enormous variety; a few of the best known are apple, curly, orange, and pineapple mint, peppermint, and spearmint. All of them are invasive and should be contained or planted in a place where they can take over. They grow from 2 to 4 feet tall, and the blooms are usually white to pale purple.

Mint flowers taste like their leaves, though they are a bit milder and have a delicate minty perfume. They can be used in custards, jellies, breads, desserts, teas, and vegetable dishes. Use whole blossoms to garnish desserts or beverages, or macerate them with all kinds of fruit. Separate the florets and scatter them over salads.

To use mint blossoms, rinse the flower heads to remove insects and shake or pat them dry. The flower heads can be used whole as garnishes, or the individual florets can be stripped from their stem.

ICED TEA SORBET WITH MINT BLOSSOMS

Use any kind of mint that you like best in this delicate, deliciously cooling sorbet. Spearmint is my favorite for this recipe.

MAKES ONE QUART

1 quart boiling water

4 teaspoons black tea or 4 teabags (A good combination is 3 parts Darjeeling or orange pekoe and 1 part Earl Grey tea.)

About 20 mint flower heads

1/2 cup sugar

Juice of 1 lemon (about 3 tablespoons)

Mint blossoms for garnish

Thinly sliced lemon for garnish

Brew a pot of tea with the boiling water and tea, add the mint blossoms to the pot along with the sugar, and steep for 15 to 20 minutes. Strain the tea through a strainer to remove the mint blossoms and tea leaves. Cool the tea to room temperature.

Add the lemon juice to the tea and refrigerate until cold. Pour the cold tea into the container of an ice cream maker and process according to manufacturer's instructions. Serve immediately or place in freezer.

If the sorbet is frozen very hard, let it sit for a few minutes and process it in a food processor just before serving until it is fluffy and free of lumps. Serve it in an elegant glass, garnished with a thin slice of lemon and a mint blossom or two. Pass your favorite tea cookies.

NASTURTIUM

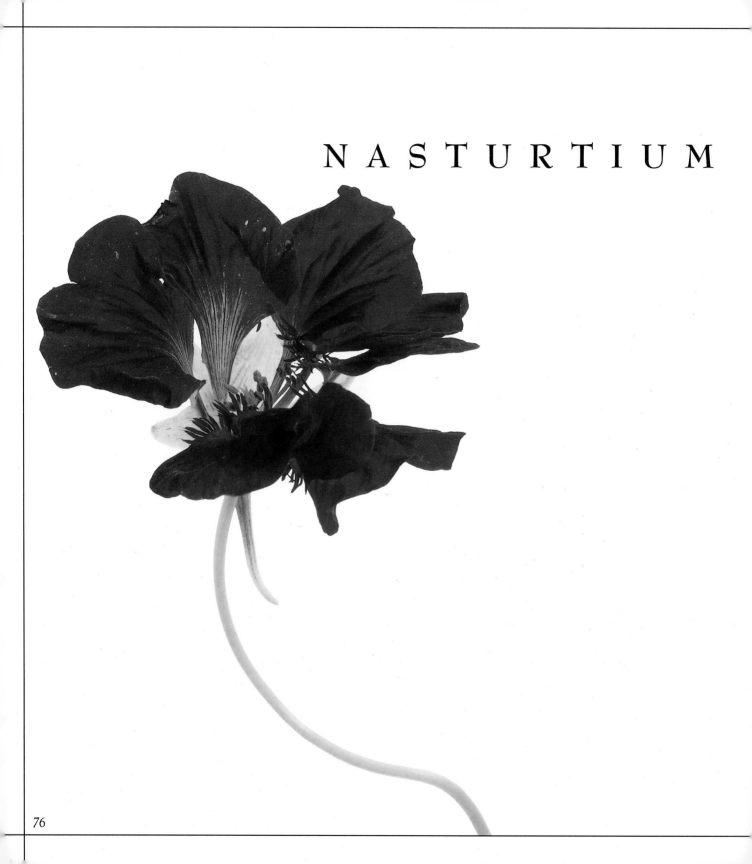

Tropaeolum majus

Sow nasturtium seeds where the plants are to grow, either in the ground or in pots; seedlings are not easily transplanted. Full sun will produce the most vigorous plants, though they will tolerate some shade. Dwarf, bushy cultivars grow about a foot tall, while climbers can reach 6 feet or more. Flowers range from pale yellow to brilliant oranges, reds, and pinks to dark crimson.

These brightly colored annuals were found in Peru by the conquistadores, who brought them to Europe. Their common name, Indian cress, refers both to their place of origin and the pungency of their smooth, round leaves.

The blossoms have the same pepperiness as the leaves, like that of watercress. However, they are milder, saladlike, and fresh-tasting, with a hint of floral scent. Over the years, I have grown many kinds of "nasties", including 'Alaska' and 'Empress of India', recommended in seed catalogs as edible cultivars. However, I find that 'Whirlybird' and 'Dwarf Jewel' are as dazzling, prolific, and tasty as the suggested edible varieties.

Nasturtium flowers make excellent containers for cold salads—egg, chicken, and vegetable—as well as cheese spreads. Whole flowers can be used in salads or as garnishes; vinegar flavored with the flowers is lovely in color and interesting in flavor. Cut into fine shreds and blended with butter, they are delicious with noodles, vegetables, and fish.

Pick nasturtiums with long stems and keep them in a glass of water until ready for preparation. Then rinse the blooms and gently shake or pat them dry. Pull the bloom from the stem and use whole, or gently tear it into separate petals. Different shades of flowers, finely shredded, make a colorful chiffonade.

NASTURTIUMS FILLED WITH GUACAMOLE

Nasturtium blossoms are a wonderful foil for guacamole because they are slightly piquant. The jicama provides a nice, crunchy base. If you don't have jicama, jerusalem artichokes are a good substitute.

MAKES ABOUT TWENTY APPETIZERS

1 large avocado, preferably
   Hass

2 teaspoons lime juice

1 small ripe tomato, very finely
   chopped

2 tablespoons finely minced
   onion

1 jalapeño or serrano chili,
   seeded, finely minced

1 small clove garlic, finely
   minced

Salt

About 20 nasturtium blossoms

1 small jicama

Lime juice

Peel the avocado and remove the pit. Mash the avocado in a bowl with a fork and add the 2 teaspoons lime juice. Blend in the tomato, onion, chili, and garlic. Add salt to taste. Let the guacamole stand, covered, while preparing the nasturtiums and jicama.

Rinse the nasturtiums carefully and pat them dry. Peel the jicama and slice it about 1/4 inch thick. Cut the slices into pieces about 2 by 2 inches. They don't have to be perfect squares—leave the rounded edges. They should be just the right size to accommodate a nasturtium filled with guacamole. Squeeze a little lime juice over the jicama slices.

At this point, the guacamole, jicama, and nasturtiums can be kept for a few hours in the refrigerator, if necessary. To assemble the appetizers, hold the nasturtiums at the base and use a teaspoon to fill them carefully with the guacamole. Set each filled nasturtium on a slice of jicama and arrange on a serving platter. The prepared appetizers can be kept very briefly in the refrigerator or served immediately.

PINEAPPLE
SAGE

Salvia elegans

When rubbed or brushed, the pointed leaves of pineapple sage have the fruity scent of pineapple and slightly musky character of sage. The brilliant, long-throated flowers have a similar aroma and taste, but the floral aroma is stronger and the sage flavor is milder. They are used in jellies, jams, desserts, and fruit salads. As a garnish, they brighten teas, beverages, tea breads, and desserts.

Cut the flower spikes and gently wash and pat them dry. The individual flowers can be plucked or stripped from the stem.

This sweetly scented sage is a tender perennial that grows into a large bushy plant up to 4 1/2 feet tall and 3 or 4 feet wide. The scarlet flower spikes appear in early autumn. If the plant is brought indoors to a cool, sunny spot, flowering will continue throughout the winter. Pineapple sage is easily propagated by cuttings or divisions.

PINEAPPLE SORBET WITH PINEAPPLE SAGE BLOSSOMS

Intense scarlet flecks of pineapple sage blossoms add a visual accent and a subtle flavor to this refreshing sorbet.

MAKES ABOUT 1½ QUARTS

1/2 cup sugar

1 cup boiling water

About 1/4 cup pineapple sage blossoms

1 large, ripe pineapple

Pineapple sage blossoms and leaves for garnish

Dissolve the sugar in the boiling water and set aside to cool. Stir the pineapple sage blossoms into the cooled sugar syrup.

Clean and core the pineapple and cut it into chunks. There should be about 5 cups. In a food processor or in batches in a blender, puree the pineapple. Stir the syrup into the puree and blend well.

Pour the pineapple mixture into the container of an ice cream maker and process according to manufacturer's directions. Serve immediately or place in freezer.

If frozen hard at serving time, allow sorbet to sit at room temperature for a few minutes, then blend or process to a smooth consistency. Transfer to chilled glasses and serve or hold in freezer for 5 to 10 minutes.

ROCKET

Eruca vesicaria

Rocket is one of the earliest salad greens of spring, self-seeding with abandon from year to year. Because it flowers and goes to seed quickly, it should be sown several times during the season to ensure a continuous harvest. Grown in

This annual salad herb, an Italian favorite, is also known as arugula, ruchetta, and roquette. Young foliage is piquant, slightly smoky and meaty, with a hint of cress; the flowers have a trace of these flavors, though milder and more delicate. As they mature, rocket leaves acquire more of a "bite". The flowers are best used as a garnish for green, vegetable, poultry, and pasta salads.

Just before use, pinch the flowers from the stems, rinse them carefully, and pat dry.

full sun, plants reach 1 to 2 feet in height. The small flowers are white with brownish-purple veins.

SPRING SALAD WITH GOAT CHEESE AND ROCKET FLOWERS

This is one of those salads that has so many good flavors that you can put together "perfect bites" from start to finish. Serve it with slices of crusty bread that have been toasted, rubbed with garlic, and drizzled with olive oil. Blossoms of regular or garlic chives may be added as an optional garnish. (This is an adaptation of an Alice Waters recipe.)

Wash and pick over the greens. If the leaves are small, leave them whole; if large, tear them into large, bite-sized pieces. Pat or spin them dry.

Preheat oven to 400° F. Cut the goat cheese into rounds about 1/2 inch thick. Cut the rounds in half or quarters. Combine the bread crumbs and 2 tablespoons chives in a shallow dish. Dip the goat cheese into the crumb mixture, coating them all over. Place the cheese on a lightly oiled baking sheet and bake for about 4 or 5 minutes.

Scrub and trim the radishes, leaving about 1/4 inch of stem. Slice the tomato and cut the slices in half.

Combine the olive oil and vinegar in a small bowl and season with salt and pepper. Taste for seasoning.

Arrange the greens on four large plates. Place the tomatoes on the greens, sprinkle them with the remaining chives, and then add the warm goat cheese. Garnish the plates with the radishes and scatter the rocket flowers evenly over the salads. Stir the vinaigrette and drizzle it on. Season lightly with fresh pepper, if desired.

SERVES FOUR

2 cups rocket leaves

2 cups lettuce leaves (try oak leaf, red leaf, bibb, or Boston)

2 cups spinach leaves

About 5 ounces goat cheese (California or Vermont chèvre or a French montrachet)

About 1/4 cup fine, dry bread crumbs

4 tablespoons fresh snipped chives

12 to 16 radishes

1 large or 2 medium tomatoes

About 1/2 cup olive oil

About 2 tablespoons balsamic or chive blossom vinegar

Salt and freshly ground black pepper

About 1 cup rocket flowers

ROSE

Rosa species

Roses have lent their light, perfumy flavor and fragrance to beverages and confections in Europe and the Middle East for centuries. The diversity of their perfume ranges from no aroma at all to overwhelming scent. Older rose varieties seem to have more fragrance than the newer hybrids. It's important to smell and taste each type of rose before using them, as some are bland and mild, while others are bitter or sour. Strongly scented varieties usually taste like their fragrance, and in general, the more fragrant a rose is, the more flavor it has. Good choices for edible roses include *R. rugosa*, *R. damascena*, *R. × alba*, and *R. eglanteria*.

Rose petals are used in making jelly, butter, vinegar, syrup, tea cakes, and desserts. They are ideal for crystallizing and are good macerated with wine and fruit. They are also used to garnish desserts and salads.

To prepare flowers for kitchen use, rinse them and shake off the water. Grasp the open flower in one hand so that the stem is pointing upward. With a sharp pair of scissors, snip right below the stem, and the petals will fall freely. Trim off any bitter white part at the base of each petal. A word of warning: hothouse roses have most likely been sprayed, and aren't suitable for use in the kitchen.

Roses have a long list of cultural requirements. They need a minimum of six hours of sun daily; afternoon shade is preferable to shade in the morning. Fertile, friable soil, good drainage, some insect and disease control, mulch, and good air circulation are also necessary. If the summer is dry, they need plenty of water, and if winters are cold, they need protection. Color and bloom time of these perennial shrubs vary according to variety, and these range from 1-foot miniatures to climbers that can grow up to 20 feet.

DROP SCONES WITH ROSE PETALS AND PISTACHIOS

These are a bit more exotic than your everyday scone and they are drizzled with a rose icing for a more dominant rosy flavor. If you prefer to serve them in a more traditional manner, pass very lightly whipped cream and rose petal jelly as accompaniments.

MAKES ABOUT TWO DOZEN SCONES

2¼ cups unbleached white flour

2 teaspoons sugar

3/4 teaspoon salt

2 teaspoons baking powder

1/2 teaspoon baking soda

2 to 3 pinches cinnamon

4 tablespoons unsalted butter

1/3 cup shelled pistachios, lightly toasted and coarsely ground

1 cup cream

1 teaspoon rose water

A good handful of rose petals

1 cup confectioner's sugar

1 tablespoon rose jelly or 1 tablespoon red currant jelly mixed with about 1/2 teaspoon rose water

Preheat oven to 425° F. Combine the dry ingredients in a large bowl and blend thoroughly. Cut in the butter until the mixture resembles a coarse meal. Stir in the pistachios.

Stir the cream together with the rose water. Rinse the rose petals and pat them dry. Shred them finely; there should be about 2 tablespoons. Stir them into the cream, then stir the liquid into the dry ingredients to form a soft dough.

Drop the dough by heaping tablespoonfuls onto an ungreased baking sheet. Bake the scones for 10 to 12 minutes or until golden brown. Prepare the icing while the scones are baking.

Combine the confectioner's sugar, jelly, and 2 teaspoons water in a small bowl and whisk until smooth. Add another teaspoon water if icing seems too thick—it will melt a little if applied while the scones are warm.

Remove the scones to a baking rack to cool slightly before drizzling them with icing. They are best served warm, right after baking.

If preparing them in advance, cool completely without icing and store in an airtight container. Wrap them in foil and gently reheat at 325° F for 10 to 15 minutes. Drizzle the icing over them while they are warm.

ROSEMARY

Rosmarinus officinalis

This tender perennial herb grows like a shrub in Mediterranean climates, attaining as much as 6 feet in height and 8 feet in diameter. Most varieties can't tolerate freezing temperatures, though, and must be brought indoors in the winter. Rosemary needs good drainage and light; without full sun it's not likely to bloom. Bloom times vary according to variety; prostrate rosemary flowers off and on throughout the year.

Older plants, those with woodier stems, tend to produce more flowers. Colors vary from blue to white to pink. Usually there are only a few flowers on a plant at one time.

Rosemary is noted for its distinctive resinous flavor, an important traditional accompaniment to meat, fish, and fowl as well as earthy vegetables and even some fruits and beverages. Flowers taste much like the foliage but milder, with a light resinous and slightly floral flavor. These delicate flowers are especially tasty with fruits and whipping cream. They can also be used to garnish salads, beverages, and desserts as well as tea sandwiches and herb breads spread with cheese.

To prepare rosemary flowers for the kitchen, cut them with the stems on and keep them in water until ready to use. Gently pinch blooms from the stems, rinse, and pat them dry.

FRESH BERRY AND ROSEMARY FOOL

Any fresh, ripe berries can be used—black or red raspberries, blueberries, boysenberries, huckleberries, or currants. If they are tart, use the extra table-spoon of sugar; if they're sweet, use the lesser amount.

SERVES FOUR TO SIX

1 cup whipping cream

2 to 3 tablespoons vanilla sugar

1 cup raspberries

1 cup blueberries

About 2 tablespoons rosemary
   flowers

Begin to whip the cream; when the cream begins to thicken, whisk in the sugar and most of the rosemary flowers. (Reserve enough flowers to scatter a few over each serving.) Continue whipping the cream until it is soft and fluffy, but not quite stiff.

Fold in the berries and chill for 30 minutes before serving. Serve the fool in elegant glasses garnished with the reserved flowers. A piece of light sponge cake or a ladyfinger is a nice accompaniment.

RUNNER BEANS

Phaseolus coccineus

Runner bean flower colors include bicolored, white, salmon, and orange. The scarlet runner bean is by far the most brilliant and the most popular. The bright flowers stand up well and make a good, sturdy garnish. The beans themselves might be green or purple; purple ones change to green when cooked.

Green-tasting with a bit of crunch, the flowers are like a mild raw bean with floral overtones. They're a nice garnish for salads, soups, sandwiches, and vegetable dishes. I like to use them to accent cooked beans and bean salads.

Cut the flowers with stems, rinse, and pat dry. Pinch the bloom from the stem and use whole.

This perennial vine from tropical America must be grown as an annual in temperate climates. It produces flowers throughout the summer followed by edible beans. Like other types of beans, it needs full sun, adequate water, and good, fertile soil. Provide a trellis, fence, or some sort of support for the vines to run up. They can easily creep to 6 feet.

HERBED BEAN SALAD WITH SCARLET RUNNER BLOSSOMS

Using half yellow wax beans and half green beans would make this salad lively with color. It can be made in advance and refrigerated; allow it to come to cool room temperature before tossing in the flowers and serving.

SERVES SIX

1¹/₂ pounds snap beans, topped, tailed, and halved

1 medium shallot, finely minced (about 2 tablespoons)

3 tablespoons lemon juice

About 1/4 cup olive oil

1 heaping tablespoon minced parsley

1 tablespoon minced basil

1 teaspoon minced tarragon

Salt and pepper

About 1/2 cup scarlet runner bean blossoms, rinsed and patted dry

Blanch the beans in lightly salted boiling water for 3 to 4 minutes or until crisp tender. Refresh under cold water and drain well.

Prepare the vinaigrette while the beans are cooking. In a small bowl, stir the lemon juice, shallot, and olive oil with a fork until blended. Add the herbs, about 1/4 teaspoon salt, and freshly ground pepper to taste. Stir well.

Pour the vinaigrette over the warm beans and toss well. Add a little more olive oil if necessary. Cool to room temperature. Toss the blossoms in just before serving the salad.

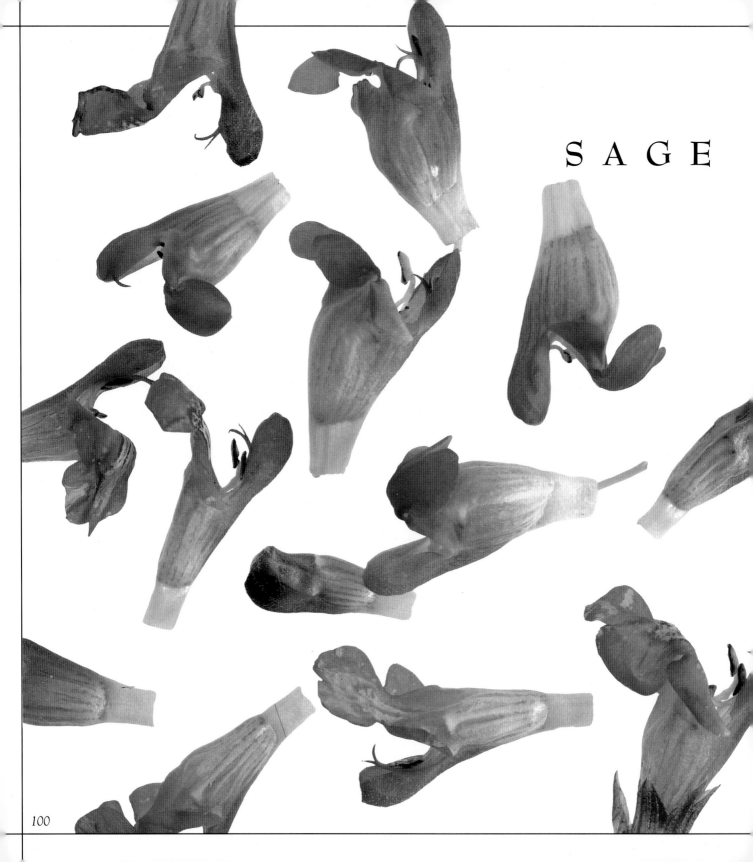

Salvia officinalis

T he pungent, musky flavor with a hint of lemon that dominates sage leaves is echoed in the flower in slightly sweeter, milder form. Sage blooms abundantly in June, making a lovely show in the herb garden or perennial border. The flowers are especially nice floating in a cup of hot tea. Use them to garnish tea sandwiches, soups, salads, and stews. Cook them in breads, stuffings, and fritters or add them to rice, egg, or cheese dishes.

Cut the flower spikes and keep them in water until ready to use. Rinse them gently and pat dry. Snip or pinch the florets from the stems.

Sage is a shrubby perennial herb that has pale gray-green leaves and blue-purple flower spikes. White- and pink-flowered cultivars are available. These hardy plants prefer full sun but will tolerate some shade. An established plant can reach a height and width of 2¹/₂ feet. Plants tend to get woody and to die out in the middle after a few years, but new plants are readily started by root division or from seed.

RICE FRITTERS WITH SAGE FLOWERS

These are really a sort of cross between a fritter and a pancake, as they are not deep-fried. Serve them as a vegetarian entree or as a side dish with roast pork.

MAKES ONE DOZEN 2½-INCH FRITTERS

1 cup cooked white rice

1 cup cooked wild rice

3 tablespoons finely minced onion

2 tablespoons unbleached flour

1 teaspoon baking powder

2 tablespoons parmesan cheese

2 extra-large eggs

Salt and pepper

About 1/2 cup sage blossoms

Oil for frying

In a mixing bowl, combine the white and wild rices with the onion and toss well to mix. Sprinkle the flour, baking powder, and parmesan over the rice mixture and toss well.

Heat a griddle with about 2 teaspoons oil over medium heat. Beat the eggs in a small bowl with some salt and pepper and stir into the rice mixture. Add the sage blossoms and toss lightly.

For each fritter, drop about 2 tablespoons of the mixture onto the hot griddle, pressing down on the top to flatten it a bit. Cook about 2 minutes on each side, or until a nice golden brown. Serve immediately.

SCENTED
GERANIUMS

Pelargonium species

These tender perennial herbs are frequently grown as house plants in colder regions. Potted specimens can be moved in and out as the weather permits. They grow best in full sun but will tolerate some shade, and they need a well-drained growing medium. Some plants reach 3 to 4 feet in height and width. As they have a tendency to get leggy, pruning is recommended.

Scented geraniums bloom sporadically throughout the year depending on the variety, climate, and growing conditions. Colors of different varieties include white, yellow, pink, salmon, lavender, and red.

All flowers from the large genus *Pelargonium* can be eaten; however, I've found only the scented ones to be palatable. The blooms have mild, pleasing scents and sometimes taste slightly sour. Lemon geraniums have a citrus flavor, rose geraniums taste perfumy and roselike, while nutmeg and ginger geraniums taste of those spices.

Scented geranium flowers are excellent for candying. They are used in all sorts of baked goods from teacakes and breads to cookies and cakes. Their sweet perfume adds flavor to jellies, sauces, custards, ice creams, and fruit salads. Use them to garnish desserts, beverages, and salads.

To use the blooms, pinch them from the stems just before using, rinse gently, and pat dry.

SCENTED GERANIUM CAKE

You may vary the flavoring according to the type of geranium blossom you are using. For instance, with lemon-scented blossoms, use the called-for lemon zest; with lime-scented, substitute lime zest. With nutmeg or clove-scented flowers, omit the zest and add 1/2 to 3/4 teaspoon freshly ground nutmeg or ground cloves. Rose geranium sugar or a few drops of rose water may be added to a cake containing rose geranium blossoms.

MAKES ONE CAKE 13x9x2 INCHES

About 24 scented geranium blossoms (a few small leaves can be used also)

6 extra-large eggs

4 extra-large egg yolks

2 cups sugar

2¹/₂ cups unbleached white flour

1/2 teaspoon salt

16 tablespoons unsalted butter, melted

Zest from 1 lemon, or other appropriate flavoring

Rose geranium- or vanilla-flavored sugar

Preheat the oven to 375° F and generously butter and lightly flour a 13-by-9-by-2-inch baking pan. Arrange the geranium flowers and leaves in the bottom of the baking pan.

Combine the eggs, yolks, and sugar in the bowl of an electric mixer and beat until pale yellow and very thick. Sift the flour with the salt three times.

Slowly fold the flour into the egg mixture, a third at a time. Carefully fold the melted butter into the batter in thirds. Fold in the lemon zest.

Carefully pour the batter into the pan over the flowers and leaves. Bake the cake in the center of the oven until the top is a pale golden brown and a cake tester comes out clean, about 35 to 40 minutes. Do not overbake.

Cool the cake completely before removing from the pan. Sprinkle the inverted cake lightly with rose geranium or vanilla sugar.

Serve plain or with whipped cream if desired, garnish with a fresh geranium flower or leaf.

S Q U A S H

Cucurbita species

The golden-orange blossoms from these annual vegetable plants are a summertime treat. Flowers of all types of squash—zucchini, yellow crookneck, pattypan, winter squash, and pumpkin—can be used, though they vary a little in size and time of bloom.

Squash blossoms taste a bit like raw squash, with a vague flowery smell. An Italian specialty is squash blossoms stuffed with cheese and fried in a light egg batter, or they can be stuffed and baked. They are delicious sautéed at the last minute with squash dishes, eaten alone, or tossed with pasta. Finely shredded or whole squash blossoms can be added to egg dishes, stir-fries, soups, vegetables, and salads.

Most varieties of squash are easy to grow—just poke a few seeds into fertile garden soil in a sunny location, water well, and stand back. Plants produce both male and female flowers. The squash fruit grows from the base of the female flower; a small fruit will already be present when the flower opens. If you have an abundance of squash and want to slow down production, harvest both male and female blossoms; otherwise, harvest mostly male flowers, leaving a few in the garden for pollination.

With a sharp knife, cut the male flowers, leaving a few inches of stem; cut the female flowers below or above the fruit. Flowers on stems can be stored in a glass of water until ready to use, or prepared flowers can be kept in the refrigerator between damp paper towels for a few hours. To prepare them, snip the stem close to the flower or cut the flower from the base of the fruit. Rinse flowers carefully; they often have insects inside. Remove the stamens and pistils and gently pat the corolla dry.

FRIED SQUASH BLOSSOMS

At the height of the season, I've seen an average adult easily consume a dozen of these during one meal.

MAKES SIXTEEN BLOSSOMS; SERVES FOUR AS A SIDE DISH

16 squash blossoms

About 4 ounces mozzarella cheese

1 extra-large egg

1 tablespoon water

1 tablespoon olive oil

About 1 cup unbleached flour

Few pinches salt

Vegetable oil for frying

Lemon wedges for garnish

Gently wash the squash flowers, remove the stamens or pistils, and pat the blossoms dry. Cut the mozzarella into 16 pieces about 1½ inches long by 1/2 inch square and place a stick inside each blossom.

In a shallow bowl, lightly beat the egg with a fork. Add the water and olive oil and blend well. Add the flour and salt and combine well to make a smooth batter.

Pour the oil into a skillet so that it is about 3/4 inch deep and place it over moderate heat until a faint haze forms on the oil.

Holding the flower by the open end, dip it into the batter and carefully lower it into the hot oil. Repeat with a few more flowers. Turn them gently so that they turn golden brown all over. Remove them with a slotted spoon and drain them on paper towels while frying the rest. Serve hot with lemon wedges.

If you are frying a lot of flowers, you can hold them in a preheated 300° F oven for a short time, but they are best if served immediately.

SWEET WOODRUFF

Galium odoratum

This fairytale ground cover is often found in woodland gardens. It is a perennial herb that thrives in the shade and spreads fairly quickly both by root and by seed. The bright green whorled leaves grow on 6- to 8-inch stems and have tiny white starry blossoms in the mid to late spring.

Sweet woodruff leaves have very little scent unless they are dried or infused. Then they give off a delightful aroma that has been described as a combination of new-mown hay and vanilla. The origin of this scent is coumarin, which is also found in sweet grass and sweet clover. The flowers have more fragrance than the leaves, though it is very mild—a hint of vanilla—and a sweet, slightly floral, grassy taste.

Sweet woodruff flowers are a favorite for the punch bowl; they are an age-old May wine herb. Use them to garnish tea cakes, desserts, fruits, and salads. They have special affinities for strawberries and rhubarb.

To harvest the flowers, cut sprigs and keep them in water. Pinch the flowers from the stems just before using.

BERRIES WITH SWEET WOODRUFF

This recipe can be made with any one of the following berries or a combination: strawberries, raspberries, and blueberries. Use a good-quality, not-too-sweet Asti Spumante.

SERVES SIX

2 cups ripe strawberries

1 cup raspberries

1 cup blueberries

1 handful sweet woodruff sprigs

1 bottle Asti Spumante

1 large handful sweet woodruff blossoms

Rinse the berries and drain well. Halve the strawberries if they are large. Put the berries and woodruff sprigs in a shallow bowl and barely cover them with 2 to 3 cups of Asti Spumante.

Cover the bowl with plastic wrap and refrigerate for 1 to 2 hours, stirring once or twice. Remove from refrigerator 15 to 20 minutes before serving. Take out and discard sweet woodruff sprigs. Toss lightly with the woodruff blossoms, and transfer the berries and their liquid into a serving dish and or individual dishes. Pour a splash of Asti into each dish as it is served to give it a bit of fizz.

THYME

Thymus species

The taste of thyme is agreeable and compatible with many types of food. French, English, and Greek thyme have the best flavor. Lemon and caraway thyme are handsome plants, and taste like lemon and caraway, respectively, when used fresh. These flavor characteristics disappear completely in cooking, however. Creeping thymes have very little flavor. The flowers of thyme, like the leaves, are sweet and savory with an earthy aroma, though the flowers tend to be a bit milder with more floral scent.

The tiny blossoms are a nice garnish to salads, vegetables, soups, and desserts. They lend interest to butters and sauces, and are tasty with pastas and potatoes, fruit compotes, poultry, fish, and most meats.

Cut sprigs of thyme and keep the stems in water until ready to use. The easiest way to remove the florets is to hold the stem firmly in one hand and run the thumb and forefinger of the other hand down it, stripping off the florets.

This hardy perennial herb stays small—6 to 12 inches in height—and grows compactly on woody stems. It prefers full sun, good air circulation, and good drainage. The tiny flowers may be white, pale pink, or pale purple, depending on variety.

PASTA AND CHICKEN SALAD WITH THYME BLOSSOMS

This makes a hearty lunch or a light supper when served on garden lettuce with fresh tomatoes, French or Italian bread, and perhaps a homemade pickle.

SERVES SIX

1 pound pasta noodles such as rotini, shells, bows, or ziti, cooked al dente

2 tablespoons olive oil

2 cups shredded cooked chicken, roasted or grilled

About 1/2 tablespoon white wine vinegar or lemon juice

1/4 cup fresh parsley, chopped

1/4 cup thyme blossoms

Salt and freshly ground pepper

1 red bell pepper, roasted, peeled, and seeded

1 large celery stalk, sliced thinly

1 small bunch scallions, trimmed to about 2 inches of green, sliced thinly

About 2/3 cup mayonnaise

Put cooked, drained pasta in a bowl, drizzle 1 tablespoon of olive oil over it, and toss well. When the pasta is completely cool, add the chicken, the remaining olive oil, vinegar or lemon juice, parsley, and half of the thyme blossoms. Reserve the rest of the thyme for garnish. Add salt and pepper and toss well.

Cut the pepper into thin strips, and then halve the strips crosswise. Add the pepper, celery, and scallions to the pasta and toss well.

Add the mayonnaise and toss lightly until the salad is blended and lightly coated with the dressing. Chill for about 30 minutes. Taste for seasoning, adding a bit of salt, pepper, vinegar or lemon, or mayonnaise, if necessary. Remove the salad from the refrigerator about 15 minutes before serving and place it on a platter or individual serving plates. Garnish with the remaining thyme blossoms.

THE VIOLA FAMILY

Viola odorata, V. x wittrockiana, V. tricolor

Wild violas are usually found in woodland environments in shade or partial shade, but cultivated varieties perform well in a sunny, herbaceous border with proper moisture and organic matter, too. Plants don't get much taller than 6 to 12 inches. Violets are hardy perennials with large, heart-shaped leaves and blooms in various shades of purple and white with purple veins. Pansies are annuals or short-lived perennials that come in a rainbow of single colors— white, yellow, orange, pink, lavender, blue, red, and purple—and bicolors. Johnny-jump-ups, also annuals or short-lived perennials (the species is probably one of the parents of pansies), are usually lavender, purple, or yellow, or a combination thereof. They often self-sow, so they'll reappear in your garden every spring.

All viola blooms taste like a mild salad green; some are also perfumed. Violets have the sweetest scent of the group; some of them have a very strong perfume while others are rather mild. The ones with the stronger fragrance have more flavor. Both pansies and Johnny-jump-ups have a pleasing, mild taste like a sweet baby lettuce, making them an ideal ingredient in fresh spring salads.

Violets and Johnny-jump-ups are ideal for candying. These harbingers of spring are used to garnish the May wine punch bowl and other beverages, desserts, tea sandwiches, and salads. They are used in making jellies, butters, and fancy desserts.

Pick violas and put their stems in water until ready to use. Pinch off the flowers and use small ones whole. Use pansies whole as a garnish, or separate the petals and scatter them over the top of the dish.

CREPES WITH VIOLA CREAM FILLING AND VIOLET SYRUP

MAKES EIGHT FILLED CREPES

Crepes

1 cup milk

2 extra-large eggs, at room temperature

3/4 cup unbleached flour

Scant 1/2 teaspoon salt

1 tablepoon sugar

2 tablespoons unsalted butter, melted, for cooking the crepes

About 40 violets or Johnny-jump-ups, stems removed

Syrup

1 1/2 cups violets, Johnny-jump-ups, or pansy petals, stems removed

1 cup water

4 tablespoons sugar

Filling

3/4 cup whipping cream

3 tablespoons vanilla sugar

1 cup cottage cheese or ricotta cheese (low-fat is fine)

1/8 teaspoon freshly grated nutmeg

1 cup violets, Johnny-jump-ups, or pansy petals, stems removed

These crepes are a rich, delicately-flavored, pretty dessert. Any of the violas can be used to make them, but purple violets with give the most color to the syrup.

To make the crepes: Combine the first five ingredients in a bowl and blend well with a whisk. Let batter stand for 1 to 3 hours before cooking.

Brush a 7- or 8-inch crepe or omelet pan with a little butter and heat over medium heat. Pour a scant 1/4 cup batter into the pan, swirling it to distribute the batter evenly. Immediately strew 5 violas, face up, over the batter. Cook the crepe for 40 seconds, or until the edges just begin to curl. Turn it and cook for another 30 to 40 seconds on the other side. Transfer to a plate. Stack crepes on the plate, covered with a tea towel, while you cook the rest of them.

At this point, the crepes may be assembled, or they may be kept for a few hours, wrapped in a slightly dampened tea towel.

Syrup: Combine all ingredients in a heavy-bottomed saucepan and simmer over medium-high heat for about 15 minutes or until reduced by half, stirring occasionally. Strain the syrup through a sieve, pressing on the petals to extract all the liquor. There should be a scant 1/2 cup of syrup.

Filling: Whip the cream with the vanilla sugar until stiff. Fold in the cheese and nutmeg, then gently fold in the flowers and refrigerate until ready to use. Remove filling from the refrigerator about 10 minutes before assembly.

Assembly: On each dessert plate, lay a crepe, flower side down. Place about 1/3 cup filling down the center and roll it up. Turn the crepes so that the seams are down and the prettiest flower parts are facing up. Drizzle a little violet syrup over each crepe and serve immediately.

YUCCA

Yucca filamentosa

This hardy evergreen shrub is native to the southern United States but also grows well in northern climates. It needs sun and well-drained soil. The stiff, swordlike leaves, prompting the common names Spanish bayonet and Adam's needle, grow from 3 to 6 feet tall. The large flower stalks, which stand erect above the leaves, bear clusters of showy, waxy flowers, which are cream-colored, sometimes with a purplish tinge at the base. After a crown produces a flower spike, it dies, but side shoots are there to carry on. Wherever you plant yucca, you will have more, as they spread readily.

Yucca flowers have a very slight floral scent. Their taste is reminiscent of artichoke or raw squash, and is sometimes a little bitter.

The crunchy flower petals can be eaten raw in salads or served with other raw vegetables with dips or sauces. They are good sautéed in stir-fries or alone, or in combination with other vegetables. The petals can be added to soups or stews.

To harvest flowers, pinch them from the stem. Wash them well. Snip or pinch off the petals at the base of the flower. Taste them: if they are bitter, cut away the base of each petal with scissors.

B R A I S E D   Y U C C A   F L O W E R S   W I T H   P E A S

S E R V E S   F O U R

About 24 yucca flowers

2 cups peas, freshly shelled or
*   thawed if frozen*

2 tablespoons unsalted butter

1 clove garlic

Salt and freshly ground pepper

Wash the yucca flowers and remove the stamens. Pat them dry.

Steam the peas until just barely done, pour the water off, and keep covered.

Melt the butter in a skillet over medium-low heat. Cut the garlic clove into slivers. Sauté them in the butter for about 2 minutes. Do not allow the garlic or the butter to brown. The butter should just barely begin to turn golden. Remove the garlic from the butter and discard.

Add the yucca flowers to the skillet, stirring well so that they all are coated by the butter. Cook them until they just begin to wilt, about 2 minutes or so. Add the peas to the skillet, season with salt and pepper, and toss well. Cover for about 1 minute, taste for seasoning, and serve immediately.

Bibliography

Belsinger, Susan, and Carolyn Dille. *Cooking with Herbs*. New York: Van Nostrand Reinhold, 1982.

Creasy, Rosalind. *Cooking from the Garden*. San Francisco: Sierra Club, 1988.

Diamond, Denise. *Living with Flowers*. New York: William Morrow, 1982.

Garland, Sarah. *The Herb Garden*. New York: Penguin, 1984.

Hylton, William H., ed. *The Rodale Herb Book*. Emmaus, Pennsylvania: Rodale Press, 1974.

Lust, John. *The Herb Book*. New York: Bantam, 1974.

Mabey, Richard, ed. *The New Age Herbalist*. New York: Macmillan, 1988.

MacNicol, Mary. *Flower Cookery: The Art of Cooking with Flowers*. New York: Fleet Press, 1967.

Menzies, Robert. *The Herbal Dinner*. San Francisco: Celestial Arts, 1977.

Peterson, Lee Allen. *A Field Guide to Edible Wild Plants of Eastern and Central North America*. Boston: Houghton Mifflin, 1977.

Reilly, Ann, ed. *Taylor's Pocket Guide to Herbs and Edible Flowers*. Boston: Houghton Mifflin, 1990.

Smith, Leona Woodring. *The Forgotten Art of Flower Cookery*. New York: Harper and Row, 1973.

Thomas, Graham Stuart. *Perennial Garden Plants*. London: Dent, 1976.

Index